Thoughts & Reflections For Throughout The Year

Edited by Sharon Spencer

First published in Great Britain in 2009 by:
Forward Press Ltd.
Remus House
Coltsfoot Drive
Peterborough
PE2 9JX
Telephone: 01733 898108
Website: www.forwardpress.co.uk

All Rights Reserved

© *Copyright Contributors 2008*

SB ISBN 978-1 84418 482 8

Foreword

Although we are a nation of poets we are accused of not reading poetry, or buying poetry books. After many years of listening to the incessant gripes of poetry publishers, I can only assume that the books they publish, in general, are books that most people do not want to read.

Poetry should not be obscure, introverted, and as cryptic as a crossword puzzle: it is the poet's duty to reach out and embrace the world.

The world owes the poet nothing and we should not be expected to dig and delve into a rambling discourse searching for some inner meaning.

The reason we write poetry (and almost all of us do) is because we want to communicate: an ideal; an idea; or a specific feeling. Poetry is as essential in communication, as a letter; a radio; a telephone, and the main criterion for selecting the poems in this anthology is very simple: they communicate.

Contents

Sunshine Thoughts	Rachel Taylor	1
The Door	Allan Lewis	2
Christmas Card	MC Jones	3
Paradise	Owen Edwards	4
Mortality Flies	Stuart Fowler	5
The Recipe	John William Hewing	6
For You	P Dempsey	6
The Holy Throng	Cynthia Taylor	7
Episcopalian	Irene Grant	7
The Passover Lamb	Deborah Grimwade	8
Eclipse	Roma Davies	9
The Field	Michael Thomas Hill	10
Lord I Thank You	Emma Cartwright	11
Along The Way	T G Bloodworth	12
Untitled	June Johnston	12
A Friend Like Jesus	Hayley Jones	13
Immanuel	Shirley Johnson	13
Satan's Ways	Karl Jakobsen	14
God Above	Maureen Thornton	14
The Book Of Life	Ray Varley	15
The Cross, The Cross	Marjorie Dobbs	15
Angel In Heaven	Anastasia Williams Owolabi	16
Psalm 23	Ruth Hartridge	16
Music	Deborah Gail Pearson	17
Change My Heart Lord	Joy Elaine Mendez Shim	17
God's Love	Moira McAllister Brown	18
How Life Should Be	Susan Carr	18
Lisse	Gilberto Dias	19
Tanglewood	David William Hill	19
God's Angel Stands In The Sun	Christine Shurey	20
Turn Back The Time	William Jebb	21
I Know I Saw You Lord Jesus	Anjum Wasim Dar	22
Hold My Hand Little Boy	Valerie Furbank	23
Come Set Me Free	Alan Davies	24
Untitled	Leslie de la Haye	25
When Angels Cry	Christine Ronoe Parker	26
Word Picture	Z Cole	27
Changing Their Ways	Eunice Ogunkoya	28
Prayer	Anthony McGeehan	29
Man's Nature Or God's Will?	Geoffrey Alan Chapman	30

Soul Attraction	Lisa S Marzi	31
The Stable	Tony Gardner	32
This Land	Ronald Claxton	32
Jesus	Hope Cameron-Douglas	33
Spirit Of Joy!	Simon Foderingham	33
The Moment Of Faith	Alasdair Sclater	34
Talking (Or Praying?) To God	Edilson Afonso Ferreira	35
Black December	Simon Weatherer	36
Song Of Praise	Mabel Dickinson	37
My Prayer	Anthony Rosato	38
Dawn Of Hope	Vaughan Stone	39
St Peter's Palgrave	Steve Glason	40
Jesus Is My Saviour	Grace Cameron-Douglas	40
Tent Of Oneness	Ruhi Darakshani	41
Turn To The Lord	Christine Wilkinson	41
From Darkness Into Light	Catherine Armstrong	42
Look Within	Christina Jones	43
Was I Dreaming?	Eddie Jepson	44
Worth Valley Sunrise	Kathleen Scatchard	45
What Is Worship?	P K Janaky	46
The Creator	Andrew Gruberski	47
God Wants Peace	Frederick Lewis	48
God's Device Intricate	Kalyan Ray	49
Have Faith In His Loving Care	Vassilia Hill	50
God's Hand	Margaret Patricia Donaghy	51
Heaven	Barry Winters	52
He Touched Me!	Colin Wide	53
In God's Hands	Norman Howells	54
Promises	Pat Bidmead	54
Came The Day	John Clarke	55
For A Nation	Timothy Cope	55
Oh Lord Creator Of Mankind	Christina Christodoulou	56
I'll Do It My Way	Albert Watson	56
Pure Love	Alan C Brown	57
Hello Jesus	Jacqueline Claire Davies	57
A Heartfelt Prayer	Francis Allen	58
The Fountain Of Life	Kathleen McBurney	59
Prodigal	Richard Gould	60
The Purpose Driven Life	Douglas Cave	61
The Olive Tree	Elizabeth Mason	62
Bright Star Of Light	Alan Knott	62
Priceless Joy	Muriel I Tate	63

Wintertime	Naomi Noonan	63
Thank You For This Day Lord	Carol Bernadette Boneham	64
My Walk With God	Rosina Forward	65
The Sacred Space	Barry Broadmeadow	66
Patience	Sylvia Quayle	67
The Garden	Ken Miles	68
Be Nice	Tricia Gabbitas	68
The Saddest Ones Of All	Tony Taylor	69
A Friend Walks Beside Me	Dave McFadden	69
Now I'm Going To Rock This Nation	Michael McNulty	70
The Soldier	Catherine Manley	71
Author! Author!	Derek Norris	72
There Is A Lord	John Walker	72
Why Do The Nations Rage?	Geraldus John	73
Hello	Jolanta Gradowicz	73
Reward	Ronald Martin	74
In The Eye Of The Beholder	Evelyn Mary Eagle	75
Assurance	Victor J Ensor	76
Forever Smiling	Ajarn Anton Nicholas	77
Perfection	Maureen Westwood O'Hara	78
I Am Not The Son Of God	David Walford	78
Untitled	Alen Ontl	79
Deeper Than The Ocean	Cathy Mearman	79
Turning Point	Sue Wilson	80
For The Loved Ones	Chantay Speed	81
For I Am The Lord Who Heals You	Deborah Nobbs	82
What Will They Say?	Brian Hurll	83
Angel	Sally Williams	84
What Is Love?	Annamarie Cope	84
Musical Dream	Josie Lawson	85
Untitled	Brenda Charles	85
Felicity	Suzanna Wilson	86
If You Can Hear Me	Sonya Nikolosina	87
Clouded	Ruth Alice Toy	88
No Sad Laments	Doreen Hampshire	88
Will We Ever Learn?	Rocie Hues	89
His Love is . . .	Shirley Sewell	89
Begging Letters	Philip Anthony McDonnell	90
My Own Angel	Victorine Lejeune-Stubbs	91
Get Through	Hugh Campbell	92

Beyond The Cross	Henry Disney	93
If My World Was A Canvas	Michael Campbell	94
Untitled	Petya Christie	95
Omar's Thoughts	John Troughton	96
Unwanted Advice	Barbara Lambie	97
Treasures Of Friendship	Susan Russell-Smith	98
Entertaining Angels	Brian Tallowin	98
Coming To Terms	Mary E Gill	99
Stories	Naomi Lange	99
The Embryo (Meant To Be)	Mike Hynde	100
Don't Let Me Die	Ann Morgan	101
The Holy Rap	Steven Williams	102
Down The Line	Irene Keeling	103
Life Rhythms	Caroline Skanne	104
The End	Donna Salisbury	104
Finding Faith	H D Hensman	105
God's Rainbow	Sue Reilly	105
Step By Step	Ise Obomhense	106
Psalm	Debra Ayis	106
Don't Give In	Violetta Jean Ferguson	107
Silence	Mary Johnson-Riley	107
So To Believe	Cecilia Jane Skudder	108
Why?	Patricia Lay	108
Breaking Point	Brenda Artingstall	109
The Loving Heart	Diana Mudd	109
Understanding	Ian Russell	110
A Child Of God	Elizabeth Slater Hale	111
Light	Linda Knight	112
Depends On How One Looks At Things	Pearl Foy	112
Happy Feelings	Diana Daley	113
Thou Art God	Imogene Lindo	113
Aging Thoughts	Leonard Butler	114
Yesterday's Dreams	Adrian Brett	114
Your New Home	Penny Kirby	115
Hope	Jackie Graham	115
Required Of Life	Margaret Burtenshaw-Haines	116
I Walked The Rugged Pathway	Andrew Blakemore	117
Mary's Song	Karen Wood	118
Freedom	Brenda Hughes	119
Easter 2008	Vivienne Brocklehurst	120

Sunday School And The Outing!	Mary Anne Clock	121
Redeemer Of My Soul	Joan May Wills	122
Treasures Of The Heart	Russell Mortimer	123
The Suffering Saviour	Raymond W Seaton	124
Far From The City	George Coombs	125
He Is Risen!	Stanley Birch	126
My Easter Wish	Mary May Robertson	126
Rock	Chris T Tanithe	127
The Atonement	Carole Ann Hort	127
Easter At St Saviours On The Cliff	Kenneth Lane	128
Love - Disposed	Colleen Biggins	128
Mary's Easter Song Of Joy!	Margaret Bennett	129
God Of Hope	Angela Cutrale Matheson	129
Easter's Fruition	Nithie Victor	130
He Was God's Son	Thomas Ritchie	131
Jesus Will Then Love You Even More	Ivar Kalleberg	132
Easter Story	Maxine A Forrester	133
Easter	Sheila Bates	134
Bible Story	Eileen Caiger Gray	135
Maytime	Mary Frances Mooney	136
God Bless You	William Ahern	136
Emmaus Revisited	Bernard Fyles	137
Spring's Promise	Joan Heybourn	137
Believe	Anne Sackey	138
Potters House Christian Fellowship	Teri Manning	138
After The Visit	John Barker	139
Fulfillingness	Andrew Hobbs	139
East And West	John Hobbs	140
A Rose Unfolds	Di Bagshawe	141
Life Eternal And Infinite	Helen Sarfas	142
A Rainbow Of Umbrellas	Pamela Sears	142
Lifting The Veil	Maureen Quirey	143
Early Today	Patrick Osada	143
Windows	Ramandeep Kaur	144
A Wedding	Jennifer Collins	144
So Close To Spring	Sheila O'Hara	145
Anniversary	Pauline Pickin	145
Not Our Wish	Christine Mary Creedon	146

Of All The Places	Joy Milligan	146
If You Dream	Muhammad Khurram Salim	147
Three Gold Rings	Kenneth Mood	147
Rainbow Of Despair	Alvin Creighton	148
Happiness Is . . .	Joy Saunders	149
Picasso	S Beattie	150
By Example	Patricia Taylor	150
Cupboards	Barbara Tozer	151
Sightings	Paul Thompson	151
The Baton Of Life	Rosalin Harvey	152
Ribbons	Anita Richards	152
Cefn Lea	Lozi Bolton	153
Ask Yourself	Nayyar Shabbir Ahmad	153
Coincidence	Rosaleen Clarke	154
Years Gone By	Bryan George	154
Love On Call	Roger Taber	155

The Poems

Sunshine Thoughts

The glory of sunshine
It brightens our world and lives
Cheering the weary, energising the slothful
A mighty natural source of energy
To search, to find, to want a cost
To treasure where nothing can spoil.

So much could be said of happy sunny days
All round the globe
Enhances the beauty of places
Aids growth to all crops
Ripening by nature's wondrousness
The sun and showers to value for sure.

God knew best with all He created
His warnings to heed
His message to obey
Examples untainted by mankind
His spirit shines in all true ones
No jury or judge to need.

Mankind declares a mixture to muddle
All sorts to rob, a purer thought
All kinds of sorts that tempt
Of make believe there's too much
Of conscience there's not enough
To aid by creation's way.

To say or know, stands not alone
At peace with one and all
At cost of course, to overcome
Scientists will assure a theory
Fuelling and fooling all foolhardy ones
Majority also all through the ages.

On hopes alone, not sound enough
Mistakes to make, reaps errors all
A purpose true, rewards anew,
By jingo to say, we can with will we will
Our best falls short like cloudy days
That brighter side to look and seek.

Rachel Taylor

The Door

Can you hear the knocking
Like the rhythm of a drum?
It is quiet but insistent,
It is calling out to come;
It is seeking out an answer,
It is crying out for more,
It is saying come and open
To see behind the door.

Can you see the glowing
Of the lantern's candlelight?
It is gentle but persistent
It is casting back the night;
It is lighting up the doorway,
Its gleam you can't ignore
It is saying you must follow
The one behind the door.

For He that you will find
Is the He who is The Way;
He is standing gently knocking
As He has been all your days,
He is seeking out an answer,
He is asking nothing more,
He is saying come and open
For the one behind the door.

He needs you stop and listen
In the quiet of your soul
He needs you stretch your hand out,
He cannot do it all;
He needs your heart to open,
Though there's no need to be sure.
He merely needs inviting
To enter in the door.

Allan Lewis

Christmas Card

Snow to the ground,
all mass of Christ,
the stars scatter messages
across the heights.

Rustling paper, tinsel trees,
the land as white as white can be.

Icicles and bicycles, a December done,
a new year poised - music, laughter and fun.

Morning moons, frozen themes,
family friends and nativity scenes.
Put your coats on, children say,
a walk across a winter's way.

Go to church - it's been a while,
the reverend gives a good old smile.
Congregations in the act of worship,
crowds of people - mind you don't slip!

Icy paths, branches bare,
the snowman stands and takes the air.

Envelopes red and things that are said,
the sentimental songs that are played
on these occasions.
Merry Christmas, says the Christmas card
and there's a picture drawn
with artistic persuasion.

It's like a view through a window,
across a room and through the glass,
over fields and in the distance,
by an artist's frozen hand.

MC Jones

Paradise

God is spirit so I read
Not seen by man with rarest sight
For God surrounds us every day
To help us in our earthly plight.

But late one night I fell asleep
My soul rose high above the sky
I saw a temple filled with souls
Of every race and creed oh my.

Mohammed fell upon his face
With Moslem lines of symmetry
To worship Allah in their way
To worship their creator see!

Moses climbed down Sinai
With tablets in his hand
They bore directions from his God
And made him feel quite grand.

Then He who sat beside the throne
Cried, 'Rejoice to all around'
And voices came from every side
Of shalom in the sound.

Then in the Christian group I saw
Peter, James and John
David, Patrick, Andrew, George
And man to go on.

Then rose up from the central throne
The power that made the Earth His own
All dressed up as Arch Druid Lord
Whom many of those there adored.

The crowd then chanted, 'Holy be'
To God of all so eagerly
He raised His hand in blessing so
The crowds began to homeward go.

My soul son floated down to Earth
And I awoke in joyful mirth
The sun was shining straight at me
As I regained my normalcy
I'd seen my God who holds me fast
Until this earthly life is passed.

Owen Edwards

Mortality Flies

Mortality flies
Mortality dies
The spirit leaves
Its outer shell
Those who chose good
All will be well
Hoping for godhood.

All bodies will be
Resurrected
Including those
Who rejected
The ones who chose
Opposition
We have choices, many voices,
Serve our mission.

Those who follow
Strait and narrow
Blessed are they
In our God's eyes
Riches in store
For they are wise
Who live evermore.

Stuart Fowler

The Recipe

If the castles that we build should fall
Or the mountain seems too high
Do not worry when your world's in tatters
Keep cool, stand back and count your blessings
For this is all that matters.

There is always another day
Build again and find a way
Keep your faith, do not despair
Have a quiet word with God
For He is always there.
Seek the wonder of His might
For He will show the way and
Give you strength to fight another day.

Go forth with courage
Find that other door
Open it and I am sure
Things will be better than before
This recipe improves with time
I have tried it and it comes out fine.

John William Hewing

For You

The Lord is my master
The best I've ever had
He's with me every moment
With love and joy I'm glad.

There is a yes, no other
Who paid the price of sin
And takes away disaster
In love my God I've seen.

Each morning I awaken
And love is with me too
For God is love my saviour
Lord Jesus Christ His name.

P Dempsey

The Holy Throng

Satan put your back against the wall
Satan put your back against the wall
Jesus took the Cross
That *you* should suffer loss
Satan put your back against the wall
Satan we are coming after you
Soon you're gonna be in such a stew
The doors of Hell are open wide
Soon you'll be locked inside
It's hot and red and awful
For those who are not lawful
Satan we are coming after you!
The Holy Throng so glorious
The Sword of Truth Victorious
Soon we're gonna put an end to you!

Cynthia Taylor

Episcopalian

In the back pew
Where you sat
A trifle restless
While the priest
In white cassock
With his back towards
The small congregation
Bobbed twice at the alter.
We stood unobserved
At a distance having opened
The thick heavy doors
With iron handles
To go a little out of our way
A short visit perhaps to pray
We crept noiselessly
Outside again
Unknown to you all
But God.

Irene Grant

The Passover Lamb

We spied Him struggling up the steep hill
His burden so great yet not His will.
He falls by my side under the weight of its load
My body felt numb, my blood ran cold.
A soldier cried, 'A man required to carry this cross.'
I instantly stepped out, feeling all was not lost.
As I followed Him I saw His torn back
As we trod up the bloodstained track.
I had heard that He had raised the dead and made the blind to see
What where they thinking to take one such as He?
His words of wisdom and lasting peace,
How could His life of love cease?
We reached the top of Golgotha Hill
All became quiet and still
Only the noise as they banged nails ever do deep
Into his hands and feet.
They placed on His head a sharp prickly crown
Now the crowds gathered,
The air thick with their murderous sounds.
He was hoisted high in the air,
The women beneath Him cried in despair.
I saw the blood slowly drip from His hands and feet
Little knowing that His love would the dark powers defeat.
A strange darkness covered the Earth
The crowds moved away with hardly a sound
And I tentatively asked, 'Could He be lifted down?'
Together we gently wrapped Him in grave cloths.
From deep within the women wailing arose.
We placed Him inside a borrowed tomb
In great haste for the Passover was coming soon
At the time we did not know or understand the one
Who was crucified, is the one and only Passover lamb.

Deborah Grimwade

Eclipse

The moon sails high in the cloudless sky
Her mountains clear even to the naked eye.
Then a small grey mark mars her perfect symmetry
And gradually, oh so gradually, it creeps across her face
Like a cloudy veil obscuring her familiar features
As the earth's shadow falls across her.
The night sky darkens, the stars alone are clear,
Her luminosity is dimmed until only a sliver of light remains.
Then, suddenly, even that light has gone,
The moon is hidden from our sight.
The earth in darkness mourns its loss,
The air is still and waiting.
And then - what glorious sight!
A tiny gleam of light appears,
This arc of the complete circle grows and grows
As though the moon as passed through all the stages
Of her monthly cycle to full maturity in three brief hours.

Thus must it have been two thousand years ago
When the Light of the World extinguished was
Dying in agony upon the high-raised cross
And darkness covered all the earth that day
As the sun's rays were obscured from view.
But His light would appear again,
He would rise like the moon,
Rise from the darkness of His tomb
To be a shining beacon for His followers;
And if we follow Him, our guiding light
We shall be with the risen Christ through all eternity.

Roma Davies

The Field

I walked through the field as the wind blew down on
my face. There the sun shone upon me. Birds flew up to
the sky so high, their song is music to
my ears while upon this land I stand.

I gazed up at the cross of Jesus. On a bicycle sat
a boy whose eyes softly closed to the land of nod he
went. On the fence his friends sat as they softly spoke
to folk of something. I know not what they meant.
As I turned back in the distance.

I saw a figure standing there, beside me stood a child
maybe, or could this be myself in another light or would that be
what is yet to come of me? The Lord led me into
that land of happiness. God himself stood beside me in
His white robe and sandals.

His voice spoke softly to me, 'It's not the wind that
blew down on your face, but I God the king.' There
He stood and blessed us all, then He went away again.

He toughed me as I turned whole, He stole my soul.
My secrets are known only unto Him as my flame is dim.
I prayed to Him in the church, the voices sang aloud
then carried across the valley quietly.

As I raised my head to look up, my eyes softly gazed
at the sky. There looking back at me was the face of Jesus
Himself with a sad look on it. As a tear fell upon the mat
on which I sat. He gave us the gift of life, without it we're
like water that flows down stream over the mountain top
and between the cracks.

Across the sand it bounced, into the sea it dove. There
I stood upon the riverbank as the ship crossed over to
the other side. His hand touched my head, my blood
turned cold like snow upon the road. As I climbed to the top of the
mountain to reach the top of the heavenly
skies, an echo called out to me, it was God you see!

Michael Thomas Hill

Lord I Thank You

Thank you Lord for knocking at my door,
I opened it up and let you into my heart,
you have filled me with light and promised everlasting love,
that's only the start.

My heart is overflowing,
my happy tears coursed a river down my face,
you are the one I turn to Lord,
the creator of the human race.

My life is transformed; I've turned over a brand new leaf.
All because of you Lord and my new found belief.

I should have let you in before
but my ears were deaf to your knocking on my door.

Your knock got louder; I could feel you were near,
I finally listened and then I could hear.

You were not angry that I'd never heard your calling;
You never questioned or asked me why,
never judged me on years gone by.

Instead, You opened your arms and wrapped me in unfailing love,
a love that protects and helps me to grow, thank You Lord for the love
that you show.
You are loving, gentle and kind,
You are a Lord that leaves no one behind.

Lord thank You for saving me and giving new life,
You wiped out my wrongdoings and changed me in so many ways,
You brought me from darkness and gave me light and through you
Lord,
I have been blessed with eternal life.

Lord I thank You.

Emma Cartwright

Along The Way

The road is long, the body weak
Onwards to eternity.
Journeys end, relief from pain
We seek.
Glimpses of life's story
Snippets of events long past.
Brings forth a warming smile,
Comforting.
But a mind confused
Day in, day out
This terrible affliction, Alzheimer's
Offering no respite
Are they aware? These unfortunates
The celestial city awaits.
Does the subconscious seek
The path of righteousness?
Perhaps a power, far greater
Than anything on Earth
Draws them unerringly
Through the minefields of life.

T G Bloodworth

Untitled

A verse for three occasions
Engagement, wedding, birth.
Thank You Lord our Father
For putting us on Earth
We may spend lots of money
To celebrate these three
The gift you gave us, love
And that was given free.

June Johnston

A Friend Like Jesus

A friend is . . .
Someone who is there for you,
Someone who cares about you,
Someone who will love you,
Someone who is with you.

A friend is . . .
Someone that's kind,
Someone that forgives,
Someone that appreciates,
Someone that will die for you.

A friend is hard to find
But I have someone in mind
He is all of those things
That person is king
King, King Jesus.

Why not a friend like Jesus?

Hayley Jones

Immanuel

Love lies cradled,
Love lies still,
Shepherds watch
on starry hill.
Angel voices
warm the air,
Wise men search
with fervent care.
Love lies waiting,
Love lies there
Gift of grace
for all to share.

Shirley Johnson

Satan's Ways

If I'd known where it would lead I would not have taken that road
I would not have followed the example of that hideous toad.
Back then I was young, an impressionable child
Couldn't wait to be grown to run free and wild!
Ignoring the warnings, thinking I was right
Travelling in the shadows never seeking the light.
Satan's ways turned me bitter, they turned me cold
My God given blessings to the dark angel I sold.
What I'd give if I could step back in time
To be free from my life of violence and crime.
To follow again the examples, that once, I was shown
Turning my back on the damnation I've known.
Lord Jesus, show me mercy, please set me free
Change me back to the person that I used to be.

Karl Jakobsen

God Above

How gracious
Is God's love
So rich indeed
How gentle
Are God's ways
His awesomeness above
God who hears
Many or few
Eyes like burning timbers
Glow and glow.
How great
Each bird He knows
So mighty
His wonders to perform
God who brings us
Safely through a storm
Wonders of creation
Burst forth free
God of all humanity.

Maureen Thornton

The Book Of Life
(Revelation 20.11-15)

Is your name in the book of life my friend?
Have you received Christ into your heart?
Will He be with you until your life's end
When from this world you depart?

Is your name in the book of life my friend?
Are you held safe within God's hand?
Will from this life you ascend
To Heaven's Promised Land?

Is your name in the book of life my friend?
Have you faith in Christ above?
Do you succumb to this life's trend
And ignore the God of love?

Is your name in the book of life my friend?
Is your citizenship in Heaven?
Have you a hope that is a godsend
And are your sins forgiven?

Is your name in the book of life my friend?

Ray Varley

The Cross, The Cross

Forlorn I stand
It tears my heart
It grieves my mind
My Lord, my precious Saviour died
So callously was he denied.
Ah yes, but He forgiveness gives
Forgiveness and new life He brings
To all who to the cross do come
To ask forgiveness from the Son
So let me raise my eyes to Heaven
And be among the ones forgiven
In wonder once again to see
His love for us, His love for me.

Marjorie Dobbs

Angel In Heaven

Dedicated to my gran (Mam), Margaret Young McCartney)

Ten years have passed since God above
Wanted another angel in Heaven to share her love.
God chose you Mam to be with Him
For on that day He took our angel away.

We all love you ever so much
And long for that day to feel your gentle touch.
We know you're all around us each and every day
You see and hear what we are doing for your love is here to stay.

God has taken you from us ten years ago
But Mam, your love is so deep in our hearts and will always be aglow.

We were blessed with a special woman in our lives
You were outstanding Mam and showed us an excellent example of how
To treat, respect and take everything in our stride.
We all love and miss you
More than words or actions could ever express
Cause all our hearts were broken the day we laid you to rest.

If love could build a stairway from Earth to Heaven above
Then we would through each and every one of our love.

Anastasia Williams Owolabi

Psalm 23

Goodness and mercy
Unfailing each day
The Shepherd unchanging
Attending our way.

Quiet waters of stillness
Green pastures of rest
Full cup overflowing
And so we are blessed.

Ruth Hartridge

Music

I met my Lord on a mountain top
This meeting was long overdue
With love in His eyes, He beckoned to me
And said, 'I've been waiting for you.'

The way had been long and the path had been steep
With many a turn on the way,
But now, in His presence, my tired heart took wings
And the dark of the night turned to day.

He said, 'Don't look back, all your sins are forgiven
And hid in the depths of the sea;
And all that I ask for this gift freely given
Is for you, my disciple to be.'

So I'll cling fast to that light till the end of my days
Knowing safe is His promise and true,
Secure in His arms with each passing day
In His strength there is naught I can't do.

Deborah Gail Pearson

Change My Heart Lord

Create in me a heart of pure righteousness
I ask of you God my life truly bless,
Free me dear God from all of life's deception
Deliver me from all other's perception.

You are God and God alone
You are the only God that I have known.
I know I have strayed off and done my own thing
I need you to return and take me under your wing.

Let me not stray off and return to alcoholic drink
That give false promises of peace and a mind to rethink
Oh yes, I've gone through valleys and mountains very high
It's not possible I could have lived through that
So I can look up with relief and sigh.

Joy Elaine Mendez Shim

God's Love

God is for all -
His presence is the assurance we need in this troubled world
He is our light in the darkness
In times of anxiety and anguish, happiness and joy!
Jesus walked this Earth over two thousand years ago
I wonder -
What he would think about it today
What would He say?
Would He think many had faith
Or feel we had faltered along the way.
Imagine God's compassion
His caring - loving!
I believe His being is relevant today
In this ever changing world -
God's love is for all.

Moira McAllister Brown

How Life Should Be

No football fans ever chanted His name
as He scored the goal to win the game,
no Oscar for Him, nor best-selling book,
He graced no front cover with this seasons look.

Never stood for election, never started a war,
the trappings of royalty - He never wore
and His chest bore no medals for bravery
as He hung on the cross at Calvary.

Yet for two thousand years His light has shone
from that one humble life of thy will be done,
when He sought not fortune, fame or glory,
but to show through love how life should be.

So when the bright lights of our vain world pall,
let's turn to the light that eclipses them all,
and act on His words so simple and true,
'Love one another as I have loved you.'

Susan Carr

Lisse

Burst forth oh luxuriant wonder
Of sand, clay, water and peat
Out of your hidden elements
Miraculous beginnings repeat.

The man of God is come
And the river continues to part
Creation, a harbinger of spring
A testimony of a benevolent heart.

Let the entire world gather at Lisse
For there the glorious frolic unveils
The components of dust recalled;
Retrieved from all terrestrial ails.

Let us go with the prophet to the platter of glass
And there, a prolific offering to the maker bid.

Gilberto Dias

Tanglewood

Made good
As it should
By God or nature
No past or future
Eternal, like a heavenly tree
Flowered, empowered by the honeybee
See, oh see with the inward eye
Which can fathom the infinite sky
There is room and place for all
Plenty of space
At beck and call.
If only we would realise
The prize called peace.
War would cease
And all bondage
Be given release.

David William Hill

God's Angel Stands In The Sun

The bright white angel of God
Standing in glorious yellow
Shining, shimmering sun
In Heaven proclaiming God's word
Doing His bidding wonderful.
Heavenly beings so glorious
Your loved ones, thank You Lord.
For God's son Jesus, Son of Righteousness
Mighty God, dying Lord, Son of the Risen Lord
We stand in God's son Jehovah's
Shining, glorious bright white light
Shimmering blues, snowflakes
Soft dew of God's heavenly bright.
Beautiful gold, silver, diamonds to wear
Pondering our hearts God's Holy Word
Cluster of juicy fruits, strawberries, oranges
Grapefruits, lemons too, thoughts of God's blessing
Of God in our lives, answered prayers
His healing hand too many to count
Thank You Lord of Your holy angel
Your only son Jesus living in our hearts
And lives each day and dark night
How wonderful mighty, honourable, glorious you are
Shining star of Bethlehem, Heaven of heavenly light.

Christine Shurey

Turn Back The Time

If we could turn back time, what changes would we make?
We could bring Jesus into our lives, to love, give and take.
Changes, I could make many, that would suit my stride
As we turn back time, I'll keep Jesus by my side.
The clock keeps ticking, can we turn back time,
I often wonder, while I'm writing this little rhyme.
Turning back time, knowing that Jesus is everywhere.
We are glad to know, that our Saviour is always there.
Turning back time, I know that this won't do
We've got to be satisfied, both me and you.
I think a lot of people, would like to turn back time
Regrets, what the could have done, maybe make another dime.
If we think of long ago, those were, the good old days,
We must keep thinking of Jesus, as He's there in many ways.
Turning back time, many years past, when He first arose
Can anyone remember? I doubt it, I bet nobody knows!
So if we can turn back time to when life first began
And knowing that Jesus, Son of God is a lovely man
Who died for us on the cross, so we could carry on
Turning back time, well before our lives are gone.
When I think back when I was young and in my prime
And how I said my prayers now and then along the line.
When we think of destiny will God be waiting for us all
Yes, He'll be there, don't worry when he hears our call.

William Jebb

I Know I Saw You Lord Jesus

Heavy was my heart and soul
My body stiff and cold -
I had no desire for food
Nor the will of life within
This mortal fold;
All seemed at the edge
Thick bestrewn like the Memphian sedge
My walk was like under a cross
Dragging heaving hurting,
Hoping, groping, praying,
Would I survive?
How long would I be alive?
The saline bottle shook on the stand
As the last drop dripped, the needle pulled from the hand -
And I still and listless, almost breathless
Let my eyelids free to meet
Just then I became conscious of a strong white light
Which started growing strong and bright
With great difficulty I tried to open my eyes
In trembling, flickering flashes I tried to rise
But pure calm and peace prevailed
At what I saw, I saw and I sank -
I got my answer from the Lord
Dear Lord Jesus please accept my thanks
For Your love and care
Please now accept my prayer
Help me to be good, to love and to forgive
And help and guide me to care and share.

Anjum Wasim Dar

Hold My Hand Little Boy

Hold my hand little boy - walk with me
There are so many lovely things to see
Together we'll explore as you learn a little more
About the beauty of each flower and tree
And before very long, you'll recognise the blackbird's song
As we walk along little boy.

Hold my hand little boy - don't make a sound
You'll hear the voice of nature all around
In the whisper of the breeze and the buzzing of the bees
Or a tiny leaf just floating to the ground
We might see a violet shy or perhaps a butterfly
As we both walk by little boy.

Hold my hand little boy - feel the gentle rain
Then suddenly the sun is out again
We'll watch the rainbow bright till it disappears from sight
These wonders no one can explain
With skies above so blue I feel such love for you
It's too good to be true little boy.

Soon you'll grow up little boy - it has to be
And you will no longer walk with me
But treasure in your heart what you've learned from the start
Of all God's gifts so wonderful and free
Childhood goes so fast - too soon these days are past
 But memories always last little boy.

Valerie Furbank

Come Set Me Free

Lost inside, my lonely shell
Little me, not known too well.
Oh how I suffered, as a child
I grew up meek and very mild.

I had to hide my inner pain
A million tears, suppressed in vain.
How I'd like to be alive and free
If Christ could live, inside of me.

I hate this life of violent pain
But love and peace one day will reign.
Inside us all, there's a tearful pot
Of forgotten hurt, we try to blot.

Anger blocks, my chakra flow
But pain will heal and love will grow.
Inside I sing, come set me free
For a Saviour's hand to rescue me.

Live as long as life can be
In Christ our Lord, that's eternity.
Set your sights on spiritual heights
Climb up high and fight for rights.

Set a goal of achieving tasks
Let God direct your path in unveiling masks.
Let trouble and strife be of knowing
Let the light of Christ guard your going.

You see it's plain as eyes can see
To reach the light and gain liberty.
My God, my God, it shall be done
Your will for me to accept Your Son.

Alan Davies

Untitled

To have - to give
To hope - to live
To God - we pray
To whom - each day
We are - no slave
To fight - be brave
To live - not lie
One day - we die
From war - abstain
And yet - sustain
With truth - for good
With hope - we should
Not fear - know joy
A girl - a boy
At birth - feel pain
For all - we gain
Fight on - live strong
Know right - know wrong
To laugh - to cry
Though we - may sigh
No fear - of death
With our - last breath
For peace - today
Let us - all pray
For now - and then.
We say - *amen!*

Leslie de la Haye

When Angels Cry

Who will cry for you my lovely
When life fades from your heart?
When columbines adorn your coffin
When love comes to your aching heart.
'Twas in the midst of late December
Many years gone by
When our beloved precious Jesus
Was born unto a winter sky.
Who will weep within the bower
Of a guardian angel's eyes
When the cross of all-times crosses
Over a dark and cloudy sky?
Who will weep a thousand teardrops?
Who will wail with started cry?
I shall weep my darling angels
Far across a neon sky.
For the lights of many a rainbow
Reaching out to Bethlehem
Where the new mown hay in winter
Beckons abide with me again.
Who will weep for you my lovely?
Who will cry the final cry?
I shall weep until forever
Or till angles cease to die.

Christine Renee Parker

Word Picture

I would like to paint you a picture in words
Imagine a vivid blue sky, abundant with birds.
In the early dawn a beautiful sunrise
A huge red ball adorns our skies.
Fields of poppies swaying in the breeze,
And a wonderful wood with magnificent trees.
Newly born lambs frolicking in the sun
Children happily playing, having fun.
A delicate spider's web that looks just like lace
Twinkling stars suspended in space.
Colourful butterflies with silk like wings
And toadstools in a magical ring.
Spanning our land a remarkable rainbow
There for all to see, there on show
Cool clear waters of a babbling brook
High in the trees a family of rooks.
Waves gently lapping golden sands
Lovers walk the shore, hand in hand.
Carpets of bluebells in our woods,
A rotten trunk where a tree once stood.
The silver moon in a black velvet sky
Shining so bright, way up high.
This wonderful world in which we dwell
We all have the choice to make it Heaven or Hell!

Z Cole

Changing Their Ways

When the future looks bleak and gloomy
Everyone has the potential to change their ways
If they so wish
Hopefully for the better and in the right manner
The problem is how to do so
Perhaps like that most changeable phenomenon
The almighty weather
From cold to hot or dry to wet
From cloudy to sunny or stormy to snowy
From foggy to clear or windy to still
But how do they know which way is right?
And how do they know vice-versa isn't better?
So to avoid dismay and despair
And to keep on the straight and narrow
They need to have faith
In God, the Almighty Father
To provide the wisdom, strength and courage
For changing their ways.

Eunice Ogunkoya

Prayer

They say dear God it's hard to do
Sit down and converse with You
Sing our praises, lament our woes
Confident You will give an ear to all our throes.

You certainly don't go into a huff
When at times we choose you to rebuff
Instead with words so softly unspoken
You calm my fears with fatherly emotion.

Within our chat You point the shame
Remindful thus it was our selfish blame
The good, bad, the shape rewards
In the circumstances beget towards.

It's nice to know you've a point to make
Myself included advice to take
Your message clear for all to hear
If you cannot do good, then evil steer clear.

Dear God this prayer is very nice
I think perhaps I will have a daily slice
I am now aware You have sussed me out
Sleep tonight will be without doubt.

Anthony McGeehan

Man's Nature Or God's Will?

Throughout our human evolution, before we could speak and before
    we could write
In our desire to survive as a species, we had to learn how to kill
    and to fight.
Lucky for humans we developed a brain, far in advance of Earth's
    other creatures,
This gave Man a huge advantage, just one of our many
    predatory features.
From caveman to spaceman and still we're advancing but seeking
    more powerful ways to kill
Is this just inherited human nature or is this a part and design
    of God's will?
The good Lord according to what I have read, created all of the
    Heaven and Earth
The seas, the mountains, forests and deserts, every creature
    was given a worth.
What is God's plan for the human race, are we destined forever
    to kill and be killed
Or will there come a time in Man's future when his lust for blood
    will be fulfilled?
In seeking the answer to this poems question, is it Man's nature
    or God's will?
If this isn't part of God's great plan, why does He allow we humans
    to kill?
Why do we have so many religions? Why so many gods per one
    human race?
If there is but one God I'd sure like to see Him and gaze upon His
    wondrous face.
I would like Him to put an end to all wars, the wasteful slaughter
    of all mankind.
Heal the sick; give voice to the dumb, sound to the deaf and sight
    to the blind.
I amongst others have lived through wars created through powerful
    people's greed
Desiring the land and possession of others, far beyond their
    personal need.

As far back as history has been recorded powerful people all round
                                                                     the world
Schemed and plotted the invasion of others and banners of war
                                                        were the unfurled.
I fear I may die not knowing the answer, maybe the answer can
                                                          never be known
Not unless of course I get to Heaven and get to see God upon
                                                              His throne.
If it isn't God's will for man to kill and Earth was created for all to share
It stands to reason the power mad killers in Heaven cannot go there.
Least, I hope not!

Geoffrey Alan Chapman

Soul Attraction

No one sees you like I see you -
Stripped of all your material possessions
And physical looks
You are like the sweetest perfume
Blown on the wind
To arrive at your soul destination.

You are the 'divine' body that I have been searching for
The one that brings me infinite warmth and peace.
You are like a 'fire' of desire, burning bright within me,
That can never be extinguished.
You are my soul partner
When the term 'dancing on air' takes on new meaning
And the sun, moon and stars are our stage.

You are the soul essence embodied in my spirit
And that will be eternally with me,
Because you are my soul attraction.

Lisa S Marzi

The Stable

There's always a warm and a magical feeling
Of soft living creatures and smell of the hay
The stable is special, no wonder our Saviour
Was destined in that precious manger to lay.

Jesus, the Saviour of every poor sinner
Who showed us the way that we all ought to live
Despising the wicked, embracing the goodness
And when we can do it, forget and forgive.

Tony Gardner

This Land

This land I walked when I was young
In rain and wind in snow and sun
The days were long without a care
All kinds of sounds you also hear.

This land that grows so many things
The puddles and the watery rings
Will bring the plants up through the soil
This in nature you just can't foil.

The lush green grass is growing strong
The trees in bud with branches long
The birds they sing so loud their song
And all around this peaceful sound.

The bridle path you come upon
This winding path you gaze upon
There's nature in the hedgerows there
It all goes on without a care.

This wondrous land we all do share
Throughout the seasons of the year
And no one has to look too hard
To see this land from not too far.

Ronald Claxton

Jesus

J is for Jesus, who is God in the flesh
E is for eternity where we will live and rest
S is for salvation which delivered me from sin
U is for use me Lord to spread the gospel of Your world
S is for all my sins that Jesus washed away and the cleansing that He brings.

Hope Cameron-Douglas

Spirit Of Joy!

Let all creation join in one
With hearts uplifted in love
Giving thanks and praises to Thee
Raising hands to the above.

Filled with the spirit of life
The very spirit of Christ divine
In splendour and loving praise
Within our hearts ever shine.

Let us worship Christ this day
Praising His name so deep and loving
Reaching out to the realms of peace
With hearts that willingly sing!

Glory to the Father and the Son
Who grants light and guides our ways
Teach us to serve You all our life
As You bow down to hear our praise.

Simon Foderingham

The Moment Of Faith

So many years of growing up
Rebel against the faith which in its prime
Restricted me a child to live my life according to its morals
For childhood spoke with whispered tongues
Of Sunday school and punishments undefined
So damned I the faith of my fathers
To live as an atheist in its prime
And believe sometimes in other religions sometimes none
I studied science and believed
We are just bundles of nerves

But in my mind the dread uncertainties lay
And the certainty of childhood spoke
And I began to think is there but something beyond
So one day did I go to a catholic priest
To speak the life of doubts about the incarnation of the world
In one response he said to me.

I cannot prove what we say
That there is a world beyond death
But how do you want to live your life
Do you want to live it where friendship and love do not matter?
My eyes grew dim and I began to see
And then in blinding light I saw the faith
I stepped out into the street
And passed a fox on the other way
In one sentiment I felt, I believed, I saw
And faith was back with me.

Alasdair Sclater

Talking (Or Praying?) To God

My God, why don't you come?
You, who are the creator
And see what Your creation became?
And see how Your people are living?

Maybe because I am a naive man
I am not able to understand Your design.
Maybe You had imposed this fate on humanity!
But must we venture this of our God?

I think you know probations and tribulations
For long time Your people are suffering.
But, for God, just by You who are our Father
For how much time? When and where our meeting?

Meeting of reason and faith, and passion.
End of homesickness, for whom or for what.
For the primeval wellspring that outpoured us, long long ago
For the Being we venerate and, some of us love.

For one manor house, once inhabited
In the paradise land that was relieved
Not by one, but by four rivers.
Where the manor house, where the rivers?

Where you, so far from your creature
Aside from mankind, deaf for our griefs?
Give us only one of your four rivers
To mitigate and quench eternal thirst of fatherhood.

Edilson Afonso Ferreira

Black December
(For Kay Black, thinking of you ten years on.)

I've finally accepted my fate
Drifting away peacefully
Towards Heaven's gate.
Couldn't believe it could end this way
Days upon weeks upon months
In bed on my back I lay.
Friends upset when they see
This vile disease
That's crept up on me.
Not knowing what to say or do
Crying afterwards
When they really shouldn't allow themselves to.
Like a girl should do I'll fight to the end
Looking out for my friends and family
And the happiness that they send.
A beautiful picture I hope you remember
Not the pain and tears
With you just this December.
My friend Kay so much to say about you
So how come I find it tough
My last memory of you.

Simon Weatherer

Song Of Praise

I will sing of a hope full of promise
I will sing of a joy without tears
I will sing of a love without ending
I will sing of a faith without fears.
I will sing of a power full of mercy
I will sing of a truth that is kind
I will sing of a pardon for all men
I will sing of a peace for the mind.
I will sing of a grace that is boundless
I will sing of a friendship sincere
I will sing of a glory so wondrous
I will sing of promise so clear.
I will sing of a courage that's noble
I will sing of a patience so rare
I will sing of a praise that is worship
I will sing of a sigh that's a prayer.
I will sing of a pity so tender
I will sing of a judgement that's true
I will sing of a freedom that's righteous
I will sing of a life that is new.
I will sing of the lamp that shall guide me
I will sing of the light that it brings
I will sing of the voice that shall lead me
I will sing of the King of kings.
I will sing of a person so vital
I will sing of a presence so near
I will sing of a spirit so constant
I will sing of my Saviour so dear.

Mabel Dickinson

My Prayer

You bring light in the shadow of darkness
You give love in the absence of care
You share no challenge in forgiveness
Nor in the nourishment of life you share
You please by knowledge and wisdom
You are strong so the weak may lean
You heal by God's enduring power
By the grace of the Lord, you gleam.
Your prayer is always solid and gold
Your silent words they speak
Your Heaven is a place so old
To keep the soulful meek.
I hold you in my heart each day
I hold you in my prayers
My thoughts for you are growing sound
Until I climb those heavenly stairs.
Your love has touched within my soul
Your gift has found my truth
Of who I am in tomorrow's world
As your steeple is my roof.
You shelter me from the hardest storm
Your open your door with grace
May love always reach you warm
In God's tenderness each day to face.
I thank you for your holy words
I thank you for my soul
I thank you for all you are.
And the strength to make me whole.
With freedom from all illness
Nothing endured infirm
May Jesus be the guide of love
To extinguish Hell's fires that burn.
May we see and know no evil
May we open our hearts to share
So the offering of our souls in life
Is traversed without despair.

Anthony Rosato

Dawn Of Hope

Auras of fear ring the shoulder of each
When stealthily summoned to share that last meal;
Anxious the glances, precluding all speech,
Expectant yet dreading what He might reveal.
Tenderly shared are the wine and the bread -
But scarce an hour later the diners are fled.
Overwhelmed by trepidation!

Stricken the shepherd, the sheep are all scattered;
Ridden with guilt are the claims of the brave.
All protestations of courage are shattered,
Each fears the shadow of scaffold and grave.
One lonely figure skulks far in the rear,
Trembling, remorseful and gutted with fear.
Peter, locked in isolation.

Huddled there in mournful silence
Each avoids the other's glance,
Scared themselves to suffer violence
From the hate that law demands.
Hard the guilt and grief to bear,
Shot right through with dull despair.
Gnawing, aching desolation.

Cool the morning, still the air,
Scent of spices, empty tomb;
Hope revives to oust despair,
Doubt is fading, faith in bloom.
Wonder, joy dissolve the dread -
Christ is risen form the dead!
Death's defeat, love's vindication.

Vaughan Stone

St Peter's Palgrave

Upon my walk one afternoon
I spied a church, oasis, calm
A haven from the summer heat
Bathing gardens, village green.

I prayed a while in utter peace
For harmony throughout the world
And those who have been bereaved
Compassion from a loving Christ.

Outside a man was clearing grass
Mowing round the ancient tombs
An avenue of Irish yews
Led me back to busy road.

There I rejoined a beaten path
Crossing bridge by Waveney stream
Savouring those precious hours
In silent worship with the Lord.

Steve Glason

Jesus Is My Saviour

Jesus is my Saviour
I love Him every day
He came from Heaven
And died that I may live.

Oh Jesus is my saviour
What a loving God He is
He put on flesh
And did His best
To give me life again.

Jesus is my Saviour and a loving Father too
He left His golden throne and praises
To be mocked, beaten and killed.

Grace Cameron-Douglas

Tent Of Oneness

In the top of mountain high
In the midst of the cloudy fog
I can see the sun of reality
The light of oneness and harmony
In the depth of valleys
In the edges of the unknown roads
In the centre of dark and misty jungles
And in the beautiful garden with colourful flowers
I can see the light of God is shining
I can hear the voice of God who calls the weak and neediest
In the tent of oneness
In the bright and happiness of the morning lights
I can see the sun of reality
The light of oneness and harmony
That calls all the nations, all the colours and all the religions
In the one tent
Tent of love and happiness
Tent of peace and oneness
Tent of life and livingness
Tent of light and safeness
And tent of oneness.

Ruhi Darakshani

Turn To The Lord

Turn to the Lord, He can still be found
Pray to Him now and make no sound.
Let all your worries and burdens depart
Pray to Him now let Him enter your heart.
And if you let Jesus make you strong
You'll have peace of mind all your life long.

Christine Wilkinson

From Darkness Into Light

Dear Lord let me start afresh with You
My new life in You assured
To begin a new relationship
With You the risen Lord
I confess all my faults and failures
I confess to You my sins
Humbly I ask forgiveness Lord
Cleanse me from evil things
To turn my back on all that is dubious
Insincere, bad and unholy
Let me be frank and clear Lord
With open heart and mind to You solely
I believe that You love and forgive me
Please Jesus come into my life
I surrender myself to Your will and purpose
Take away the anger and strife
I want to obey Your commandments Lord
Not to stray but be loyal and true
In all the things that You ask of me
In daily life in all that I do
Father I want to serve You
And feel the Holy Spirit within
Jesus please stand at the door of my life
And I'll open it and welcome You in.

Catherine Armstrong

Look Within

Have you seen God Today?
Do you now he's there?
Are you searching high and low?
Do you really care?
Don't go looking in your church
Or in your chapels too,
You must go and look within yourselves
Search within through and through.

Divine love is our God
He is the soul of souls.
God will help us through our life
To reach our many goals.
We must believe in this and that
But *faith* is the true key
Love is the universal word
So let's love and let it be.

Let's thank God for all we have
And all we have to come.
We'll climb those mountains and those hills
And when the day is done
We'll sit down calm and be at peace
And know we've done our best
Let's say a prayer to God within
And now, it's time to rest.

Christina Jones

Was I Dreaming?

One night as I lay in my bed
An angel appeared
And above her head
Shone a ray of light
The likes of which
I had never seen before.
And she smiled at me
As she pointed towards
My bedroom door
I was unafraid
I know not why
But I followed her
Down the stairs
And through the front door
Then she held my hand
And we gently floated towards the sky.
We glided peacefully amongst the stars
And beyond the moon
And miles past Mars
Would this journey
Never end?
'Is this real?'
I asked my friend.
And with a reassuring smile
She turned and looked at me
And softly said,
'You are now free
You are an angel
Just like me.'

Eddie Jepson

Worth Valley Sunrise

Sky, vermillion,
With rose,
Reflected in windows,
Mirrored,
In passing cars
Like a glow,
From planet mars,
A visitation?
Could it be
A blessing for advent,
Or some other portent,
For exultation
Or just the rising sun
A winter's day begun
Beautiful, but yet,
Was it a warning
A vision or a threat?
A local scene
No more,
Yet different from before
Subtle,
In atmosphere
Tinged with hope
Both that and fear
Brought speculation.

Kathleen Scatchard

What Is Worship?

Who is the God? Where does he live?
Why do we need a God in our life?
When you are drowned in sorrow or danger,
Is he a friend in need to give relief?
You call him for help by worship and prayers,
Worship is the boat and prayer the oars,
That take you safely to the country of the God.
Where violence is absent and all are happy,
Basking in the sunshine of eternal bliss,
But what is true worship or prayer real,
Is it fasting or a sojourn to holy shrines,
Or visiting temples mosques and churches?
Or routine ritualism, the holy entertainments?
True worship is service to the needy.
It is easy to please the almighty God,
Every noble action or thought that is kind,
Is a flower at His feet in true worship.
A selfish cruel deed pierces Him deep.
Violence and hatred are decaying dirt,
Thrown at his face, for He is everywhere,
Manifesting in known and unknown things.
Worship Him with noble thoughts and deeds,
He is a magnet, around whom all revolve,
In different orbits according to your deeds.
The farther you are the attraction least.
Get near Him through service to His creatures,
The final leap that lands you in his bosom,
Is the reward of your service to the weak and poor.

P K Janaky

The Creator

Dear God You are the heart of my life
In humbleness I praise Thee
You, the creator of everything
Of what's gone, now and yet to be;
I am but one person
In this infinity of time and space
Negligible and you still
Afford me Your precious grace.
You give me air to breathe
You give me night and day
Of water and bread to partake
Sight and hearing to convey
Touch, taste and sense of smell
The ability of thought
Power to walk and talk
These Lord, You have me taught.

Dear Father, bless me with the conscience
To abide with appreciation
To know You hold me in Your hand
At Your mercy, for salvation
To acknowledge You and You alone
Have me ever comprehend
That You are alpha and omega
You are, the beginning and the end.

Andrew Gruberski

God Wants Peace

No resources have I
As I sit on my bed and sigh,
Alive, but only just,
Will I die soon or will it be a life of lust?

The battle has not been won
Bombs everywhere in this city
Are we all doomed to die?
Let us make ourselves pretty.

We read and watch TV and wait
For news of peace to come,
The whole world has gone mad
Fighting in the rain and sun.

Politicians! Have they the answer?
Lay down your arms a bit faster.
Millions killed without a reason
Glorify Jesus and God in the new season.

To kill is all they know
Just like the Second World War
No love, no sex
All of that is gone.

One man could save us
And that is Christ
Oh, Father in Heaven
Are you still alive?

Be at peace with yourselves
While the wars rage
Put on your clothes
Got to work and save.

Many people I know beg
Some stand on one leg
Others yearn for the keg.

Frederick Lewis

God's Device Intricate

Untamed wind at times chase
The clouds dark and deep,
Sailing along the crimson Heaven;
Soon the declining splendour
Of the sun reveals;
The day rolls into night
And the unmoored patches of clouds
Look like the furies of warships,
Moving at random along
The turbulent ocean vast!
After hours the ocean restor'd
Peace and silence profound.
The crescent moon is up
Above the upright far-off hills;
They look wizard amid faint beams
Gleaming and enchanting;
The whole of the sandy beach appears
Painted silver in the drowsy beams
Soft, flooding all o'er;
Soon the army of stars appear
Spreading a sort of heavenly music
So harmonizing and elevating!
The beach appears to expand
Under the moonshine strange and animating
That invites children and birds alike;
Larks rising from the broomy lea,
Forget all about their homes,
And come down to share the joys
Of children playing, singing
And clapping their hands
In the infinity of love and amusements;
This makes the earth our hermitage
A cheerful changeful page
A God's bright and intricate device.

Kalyan Ray

Have Faith In His Loving Care

When we feel very low and in despair
In pain, fear and full of tears
The Saviour holy Lord will answer our call
If we believe in His word
He will heal all our ills and banish our fears.

But only if we believe in Him
And have faith in His loving care
We can look forward to a brighter world
Where there is no pain or despair
Only his love, his care to share.

For I know well Jesus cares for me
He'd never forsake me
When in grief, I lost the will to live
He came to me when I called to Him
In my despair and gave me strength and life
He lifted my darkness and gave me light.

Yes, the Lord appeared personally to me
And gave me the will to live
For I know that my Saviour Jesus
My redeemer lives
With love and faith in the Lord
He will answer our call.
Our Saviour, our light, our healer
Holy Lord, amen.

Vassilia Hill

God's Hand

As you travel through life
And troubles befall you
Just turn to Jesus
With all your heart
Then you'll be able to see
Your way through
Leaving all in God's hand.

He'll never forsake you
No matter what comes
He'll be right beside you
All the days of your life
He'll be there in trouble and strife
Leave all in God's hands.

Know that things only
Last a little while
His love lasts forever
Don't panic, don't be afraid
Turn to Him always
Leave all in God's hands.

Then you will see the sunshine that must follow
As you keep close to Him
Welcome tomorrow
You will see you stay close to Jesus
Everything will turn out right
Leave all in God's hands.

Margaret Patricia Donaghy

Heaven

Shimmering colours of every hue
From darkened corners, escape and flee
Dancing pictures come to life
In Heaven, even the blind will see.

The cuckoo's call, the hoot of the owl
Crashing waves seem so near
Soothing music, once forgotten
In Heaven, even the deaf will hear.

Flowing word, soft and tender
Poems of love, so beautiful, so sweet
An open heart to tell the world
In Heaven, even the dumb will speak.

Leafy lanes, sun glinting through
Gently strolling in the park
Laughing at the drops of rain
In Heaven, even the crippled will walk.

No more the sound of marching feet
Or if the bombing will ever cease
The time is now, for always and ever
In Heaven, there is forever peace.

The tears have gone, the eyes are sad
Nothing will ever be the same
You come to terms with being alone
In Heaven, there will be no pain.

Just for a moment, close your eyes
For your very best thoughts to be free
For everything you hoped and prayed for
Heaven is, what you want it to be.

Barry Winters

He Touched Me!

He should never have touched me
    I was ringing my bell,
    and shouting out, 'Unclean, unclean!'
    making sure everyone knew,
    I was sounding my death knell.

He should never have touched me,
    He should have kept clear,
    there are rules about lepers,
    they say you can catch it,
    if you get much too near.

But then this man was Jesus,
    He often broke rules,
    upsetting the Pharisees,
    working on holy days
    and calling them fools.

He should never have touched me,
    but I asked for His aid;
    I wanted to live in the town
    to go to the temple,
    like others and not be afraid.

He should never have touched me,
    but He reached His hand out,
    and I felt the sores leave,
    my shrivelled arms grow,
    and I cried and I hugged him
    and He swung me about.
I am glad that He touched me.

Colin Wide

In God's Hands

God, who joined this couple
Keep them in your care
Teach them all the good things
That are abundant everywhere.

Help them keep their pledges
Taken in Your church today
Show them patience and forbearance
In every kind of way.

With the precious ring that binds them
Keep them close and ever true,
And when they get their problems
Please show them what to do.

Through all their life of marriage
Give them many years, we pray
Let them always be so happy
Just like they are today.

Norman Howells

Promises

Dear Lord we pray,
All who kneel here today
Should see each child at the font
As an unfolded leaf,
Laying in innocence beneath
Mature blossom of our adulthood.
Let us not stray
From the duty laid upon us
In promises made,
To guide them in the way.
And to responses of we do
May we betray them not,
By breaking the vow
We solemnly make now on this
Their baptismal day.

Pat Bidmead

Came The Day

I saw the host upon the hill,
the joy of life to fulfil,
the songbirds in chorus trill.

A blazon of colour to behold,
before one's eyes a cloth of gold,
oh wondrous sight in the wold.

Came the day when a sight as this,
to blink an eye what joy you'd miss,
to stare in wonder at nature, bliss.

To walk in England's pleasant land,
adventure unfolds like Alice in fairyland,
in awe at such grandeur by God's Almighty hand.

This scene is likened to some passion play,
 would that I kneel upon this cloth of gold to pray,
that in my soul I'm blessed, came the day.

John Clarke

For A Nation

Nailed on a cross He hung there
Just to show how much God did care.

So pure and bright
In God's loving sight.

He didn't even put up a fight
To save us all
But not many will answer His call.

No more sin
No more pain
Thank You Jesus for what You did again.

Timothy Cope

Oh Lord Creator Of Mankind

Lord Creator of mankind
To Thee my soul I raise
To look upon and guide me Lord
To tread Thy path always.

Without Thy guidance I am lost
Without Thy guidance stranded
Lord, in Thee I hope and rest
Bestow on me Thy presence.

Oh Lord who loveth all mankind
Have mercy on Thy maid
And let Thy loving kindness be
My guide, my hope and faith.

Oh let Thy boundless grace overshadow me
And lead me to Thine abode
And fill my soul with burning fire
To yearn for Thee alone.

Christina Christodoulou

I'll Do It My Way

Where will you lay down your head?
In pastures green - a mortgaged house and bed
Is yours the walk by waters still?
It's motorway no time to kill
A place for you to restore your soul
Power and riches, my aim, my goal
Have you a guide along life's way?
No time for that I've bills to pay
With rod and staff climb any mount
I find comfort in my bank account
Anoint your head with holy oil
Doing that would cramp my style
Eternal home at Christ's great cost
I'm busy now - you mean I'm lost.

Albert Watson

Pure Love

Kept in the dark, we gain all being stripped
Of everything. The surgeon would need no sharp knife
If the flesh were sound. If we were not gripped
And wounded by our last enemy - the self.

Whatever we cling to too much, must be snatched
Form us; before we can enter eternal life,
Our sufferings, only when they are matched
 By cowardice are doubled, disabling relief.

Kept in the dark is gain, come leap into it,
As into the absurd, that makes no sense,
That is a place where love and faith exist,
That brings the grace of final recompense.

Kept to the other's will, avoids disgrace
And passions us, to see God face to face.

Alan C Brown

Hello Jesus

Hello Jesus, it's only me
I've not been very good today.
God bless Mummy and Daddy
And Gran and Grandad too
I've no brothers or sisters
So please bless my budgie Sue.

You needn't bless my teacher
Cos she shouted at me today
And don't bless my best friend
Cos she isn't anyway.

I really will be good tomorrow
At least I'll try my best
To be like a little angel
And not a little pest.

Night, night, amen.

Jacqueline Claire Davies

A Heartfelt Prayer

Here in our church every day
It's to the Lord that we all pray
For those who live and those who're dead
And for the sick that they'll soon mend.

Oh Lord of love and of light
Help those blind who have no sight;
We pray for the disabled and the deaf,
And all the people who are bereft.

For those who live on the street
A better life for them we seek,
That for you, Lord, they go in search
Then come to join us here in church.

We pray for those who are in peril
From dictators who're ruled by the Devil;
Those poor souls dying of starvation,
We look to you for their salvation.

There in Darfur death is everywhere;
The world leaders seem not to care.
Oh Lord help those who live in poverty
In this world that shows no mercy.

For those out there in foreign lands
There's only death near at hand;
Keep them safe, those we love so dear;
Let them live their lives without fear.

Francis Allen

The Fountain Of Life

In day to day living we give and take
We have so much to learn in many ways
The fountain of life needs to flow
Taking us on a journey we need to go.

The struggles in life are painful to bear
When stretched to the limit we are in despair
To stay on the right track takes willpower and purpose
We can learn the true values of peace which concerns us.

We all have a part to play, like it or not
Serious responsibility will no longer be fobbed off
We all have gifts and blessings to use and to share
When the strong help the weak, by this we really care.

God's wonderful creation was here when we came
We don't own anything so there is no claim.
Greed, power and selfishness would still control the nations
To our cost in the past with family and relations.

We owe to their memory a better way
Of settling our differences while we may
The colours of our skin is a blessing not a sin
We have no earthly excuse for not mixing in.

In peacetime through World War II to peace again
To take life for granted I would feel ashamed.
I do not know the answers but I know who does
God is the fountainhead of life, His love for us.

Kathleen McBurney

Prodigal

Well how long
Have I been
Sitting by the side
Of this old track
Through the seasons
Down the years
More than once doubting
A liar if I didn't admit

Just when you think
That it's a wish too far
Beyond your wildest
Hopes and dreams
Fortune and fate
Conspire to sail
Into a blurred
Horizon

Rub those tired eyes
As a soul ambles
Into view unaware
Or trying to ignore
The stirrings that rise
How long ago
Did this person
Leave for discovery

Frozen for a moment
For past cruel hopes
Before the clarity
And gathering pace
Set both toward
Each other
Years of absence and hurt
Will fall discarded

That first embrace
When feelings speak
More than any stilted words
The clasp of the shoulder
The hold of eye to eye
Tomorrow can wait with
Boundless smiles and joy
For the returning boy.

Richard Gould

The Purpose Driven Life

You were born for a purpose
The Lord wants you to know
A good purpose, to love Him
Because He loves you so.

You came to this Earth, Lord Jesus
To set Your people free
From sin, how glorious
Free to serve and love Thee.

Your purpose Lord, is my aim
Holy Spirit, please help me
By Your power, in His name
I put my trust in Thee.

How we need each other Lord
Your purpose to fulfil
That we together dear God
Will do your sovereign will.

Soon you're coming back again
To take your people home
There with You, we'll ever reign
No! Never more to roam.

Douglas Cave

The Olive Tree

In quiet contemplation I sit beneath a canopy of silver leaves,
searching for a moment of tranquillity and peace.

Above me, a myriad of precious jewels are ripening in the sun,
inviting me to stay and fix my silent gaze upon.

I close my eyes and speak to my creator through my prayers.
His holy presence capturing all worries, doubts and cares.

Resting by this tree that bears the scars of nature's sufferings,
I sense its boughs enfolding me in love and humble offerings.

These verdant fruits are but a symbol of the gifts we may receive,
when we cry, 'Abba Father', as the spirit intercedes.

Elizabeth Mason

Bright Star Of Light

There's a bright star in Heaven
I know there is
So far away but it shines so bright

Shine for me so that I may see the light.

There's a bright star in Heaven
Let it shine in that peaceful plot
Shine, so that I may be guided
Feel the warmth of your love.

There's a bright star in Heaven –
If only I could reach out and touch
So that it maybe a helmsman
Assisting others
Then my needs for this bottle would not be so great

It was the end of day
And only the night sky
Reflected the simplicity
Of what had become an anxious prayer.

Alan Knott

Priceless Joy

What I need is a joyful heart
A pure heart that can sing
A heart filled with all the gladness
That only God's grace can bring.

But am I willing to give up all else
In order to find such grace?
Will I hand over my life to the one who can keep it
At all times - whatever I face?

When I'm ready for that I shall find that 'pearl of great price'
Which gives spiritual riches each day
Then, my heart will sing with the joy of God's love
And hope will brighten every hour of my way.

Muriel I Tate

Wintertime

When piercing air turns its cold back
on winter stars, to watch the crack
of frosted grass and crispy earth,
When sea joins sky in howling mirth
and naked branches creak and moan
against the grey of barren home;

Then sharp lucidity, returning,
alleviates the hidden yearning
for all things grave and old and staid -
Now while winter's serenade
yearly comes and takes its place,
I know I'm here by God's good grace.

Naomi Noonan

Thank You For This Day Lord

How can I thank You for this day
As I kneel at my bed and pray.
Father, I know You were at my side
As my protector and my guide,
As I saw daylight appear
And as I see it disappear.
Lord is thou be my guide
As I pray for those alone
And many who have no home
Give them shelter Lord I pray
Give them peace at the end of the day.
What do I do in a world confused?
For many I pray who do not know You
Your glory will shine upon them
For Your love is oh so true
And as the clouds cover the skies
Way up there very high.
The mysteries of life Lord we'll never define
For you are so divine.
Help me rest weary I'd be
Trying hard so I can see
The glory of God let me focus on Thee
Let my mind now be at rest
Let my soul be heavenly blest
And You my Lord will do the rest.

Carol Bernadette Boneham

My Walk With God

I open my bible day by day
God speaks to me while I journey on my way.
This wonderful book is my inheritance.
Am I going to claim it with both hands
Or do I go the way of the world?
This is not what my Lord commands.

Whatever path I choose to take
The choice is mine, in life to make.
Is it going to be a venture with God?
Then I will find peace within.
Or like the prodigal son, do I go down that dark and lonely road
That leads me into sin?

I am seventy-three years of age, time is now fleeting
I am more on my way out than in.
I have been a Christian now for many years
God washed away my sin.
My dear and earthly Father was a good Christian man
And with His tender love, in my early years and good guidance
Was the time when my walk with God began.

Jesus the son of God was crucified
And He died on the cross for you and me.
On that sad day at Calvary
Until the day break.
Amen.

Rosina Forward

The Sacred Space

I open the newly painted gates
And I walk up the short slope
Towards the transparent door.
I have the keys to permit me to enter
The kingdom of God.
I am greeted with silence
As I walk quietly into the church.
I start to slow down my steps.
I feel sorry that I have kept Him waiting.
I feel sorry that the pews are empty.
All I can hear is the traffic going past
To God knows where.
People rush past oblivious of this sacred space
Where one can commune and find refreshment
For the tired soul.
I have God all to myself
But I feel sad.
I want to share Him
And allow others to feel the deep love.
To let people find the answers
When we dwell in trust and faith.
To enjoy the mysteries
And obtain reassurance.
Sometimes He talks to me.
Sometimes I don't have time to listen.
I go on my way unaware that He is within.
What can I do?
What can He do?
I'll just go on wondering,
But I find it difficult to endure his forbearance.
We all may have to wait until
The futile following of mammon is spent and exhausted.
Then may we see clearly His way.

Barry Broadmeadow

Patience

I thought about the virtues
trying to find the best
I wondered which one of them
would outshine the rest.
Most people would say honesty
and this is very true
but I also think that patience
is most wonderful too.
For patience is well needed
every single day
it helps us face the problems
which seem to come our way.
It is added confidence
to understand things more
like a kind of hidden strength
which helps us to endure.
We need patience
while waiting for springtime
which melts the snow in winter
bringing summer in.
We also need patience
with each tiny seed we sow
which when watered by the summer rain,
Earth's beauty will bestow.
We need patience if longing for
news of someone dear,
then when the moment comes,
we shed a long awaited tear.
Yet the tears shed are joyful
and not filled with regret
for that moment we have waited for,
is the one we won't forget.

Sylvia Quayle

The Garden

To my imagination came a garden,
profound in dignity and quiet peace
with solemn sweetness, hallowed mystery;
a monastery garden.

I wanted to absorb the atmosphere,
to let the mossy patina of age
infuse my spirit; let the poetry
of quietness pervade.

No sunshine cheered the garden, but a bird
wakened an echo from the ancient stones;
surely the bird belonged, its melody
possessed ethereal grace.

Sweet roses round an unmade arbour twined,
unplanted flowers fragranced all the air,
the rough stone steps were lovely in their roughness
rising from edgeless path.

Oh, could I stay for ever in that place,
shut from the world of hurry, noise and strife!
Ah yes, the ministry of prayer could rise
from that secluded plot.

Ken Miles

Be Nice

Let's make the world a brighter place
And bring a smile to someone's face.
Each day at work and leisure too
Just think of something nice to do.
For someone else to make their day
A thought, a gift, nice words to say.
And when to others you are kind
A special little joy you'll find.
That all the goodness that you do
Will come back daily unto you.

Tricia Gabbitas

The Saddest Ones Of All

We are each and every one of us sinners through and through
though the weakness Satan exploits in me is not the same for you.
In the prayer our Saviour taught us, we must understand the whole,
forgive us all our trespasses in itself won't save our soul.

As we forgive all others who sin against us too,
in this way will our Saviour forgive both me and you.
Judge not therefore lest thou be judged - don't hate or throw the stone,
though others will don't you be swayed - be prepared to stand alone.

It isn't easy to overlook the wrong doled out by others,
the hurtful words, the painful deeds from our so called sisters
                                                     and brothers.
But try to follow our Saviour's call in the life you're encouraged to live,
and remember the saddest ones of all are the ones who can't forgive.

Tony Taylor

A Friend Walks Beside Me

I was struggling to summon up, the strength to carry on
I just felt like giving in, all hope seemed to have gone.
All my many problems, I seemed to face on my own,
Wearily along the road, I thought I walked alone.
I thought no one was with me, as the road got very long,
No one was there go guide me, whenever things went wrong.
Then one day I realised why I felt this way,
So I got down on my knees and found the time to pray.
'My Lord you haven't helped me every time I've had a fall'
He said, 'My son I listened but I never heard you call.
Those many miles you travelled with your head bowed in despair
Not once did you take the time to notice I was there.'
Now I find the time for Jesus and He shares my heavy load
Now I'm no longer weary as I walk along the road
For a friend walks beside me, one I hadn't called before
But Jesus heard me pray, now I'm not lonely anymore.

Dave McFadden

Now I'm Going To Rock This Nation

Your time on Earth has been and gone
Your story still lives on
Your life was a dramatisation
Now I'm going to rock the nation.

Your story was full of pain and love
Now you look down from above
On your own creation
Now I'm going to rock the nation.

You always pick me up off the ground
So I know you're always around
You give me determination
Now I'm going to rock this nation.

I live my life so fast
I don't have time to dwell on the past.
I'm going to plot my own destination
Now I'm going to rock this nation.

Next time we're together
It's going to be forever
I hope by then I've found salvation
Now I'm going to rock this nation.

Michael McNulty

The Soldier

Woe to you who have gone before
and suffer you who come hereafter
Listen now and hear the call
not of war but of the hereafter.

Let not your call of honour and duty
perpetrate the call of inner beauty
No more death, or tears I hear
but of joy, of hope, it's near!

Look now, see now, your hope is here
In yourself beneath woe and fear.

Inner strength, victory is nigh
trust your saviour from on high.

External fight? What hope is yours?
The internal fight goes on.

Trust now, see now, what future lies
See the new dawn soon to arise.

Salvation comes, it's truth is clear
Follow, follow very near.
Be strong, be brave as all soldiers should
In the daily battle, in life, in wood.

Catherine Manley

Author! Author!

Where did this world come from, this big game?
Who is the Author of Life, whose words live forever?

Where are those who follow His book?
Love everyone, give to all who ask
Do not judge or condemn, be merciful and forgiving.
Who denies himself?

The Author of Life was killed and rose from the dead.
Be at peace with God, accept forgiveness of sins

Where is our companion?
Who strengthens our life, refreshes it with joy
Empowering us to be God's witnesses
The Holy Spirit in us all encouraging one another

Where is the Author of Life?
Exalted, at the right hand of our Heavenly Father.
Who is the Author of Life?
Jesus, the son of God, our Prince and Saviour.

Derek Norris

There Is A Lord

God acts in a mysterious way
So don't forget to pray

Without God in your life there is no aim
And you will only have yourself to blame

So if your aim in life is to go the right way
Don't forget to pray day or night
Then you will surely see the light

Come what may just make sure you do things
The right way, if you can't, try to use your head
And try hard not to be wicked

And you will rest assured
Whether you're at home or abroad
That there is no doubt there is a Lord.

John Walker

Why Do The Nations Rage?
(Chichester psalms)

Jubilant voices descending from Heaven
Crash into orchestral chattering,
'Awake, awake my soul, I will arouse the dawn.'

Man exists in his infinite smallness
God broods in his heavenly abode,
'Enter, enter into His gates without misgiving.'

The frailty of the alto contrasts
With the robustness of the warring psalm,
Why, why do the nations rage? A grim intrusion
That fails to silence the message of accord
And is swept aside by the sweet song
Of the shepherd psalmist.

With pure theatre, insecure voices mock
Man's atonal attempt to deliver
A message of vision and everlasting hope.

Hope for a world at peace within itself
Peace wherein all will fear no evil.

'How pleasant it is to dwell in unity.'

Geraldus John

Hello

I thought that the sun would never rise
And darkness would capture everything.
There are many things I should revise
My life lost sense and worth and meaning.

I thought I'd shut the door forever
 But in the time of grief and sorrow
You appeared with sunny weather
And said unexpectedly, 'Hello!'

Jolanta Gradowicz

Reward

A rich young ruler came to Jesus and said, 'To eternal life I do aspire
Please tell me how I can achieve the object of my desire?'
And Jesus said, 'You have the commandments which Moses gave to Israel,
Make sure you know them all and make sure you keep them well.'

When the young ruler received the answer, he was taken somewhat aback
'All this have I done from my youth but I feel there's something that I lack.
And the Master said, 'Go and sell what thou hast and give to the poor
For it's easier for a camel to pass through a needle's eye
than for a rich man to enter Heaven's door.'

This made the young ruler grieve and he quietly walked away
Now he knew the price of admission, he was not prepared to pay.
For he had great possessions and the price was far too high
He preferred comfort in this life rather than promises of mansions in the sky.

And His disciples were amazed and called out, 'Who then can be saved?'
For they had forsaken everything thinking that the road to paradise with treasure would be paved.'
And Jesus said, 'With men this is impossible but with God this is not so
For with Him all things are possible, this is something you should know.'

But Peter said, 'We have forsaken all and followed thee
Can you give us some idea of what our reward will be?'
And Jesus said, 'When I come to glory you will all be there as well
Sitting on twelve thrones, judging the twelve tribes of Israel.

And everyone who for my name's sake gives up things that they hold dear
Will receive their reward in Heaven when they have entered there.
This has been reserved for those who hunger and for the waters of life do thirst
For on Judgement Day the first shall be last and the last will be the first.'

Ronald Martin

In The Eye Of The Beholder

Beauty is everywhere around,
In flowers, in trees or on the ground.
Just picture a wood filled with bluebells,
Think of a beach strewn with seashells.
A rosebud then a perfect rose,
Its delightful fragrance wrinkling your nose.
Newborn lambs upon a hill,
A sunlit lake, quiet and still.
A brilliant sun in deep red skies,
Setting slowly before your eyes.
Wild primroses appearing under a hedge,
A babbling stream full of sedge.
A kingfisher hovering over a fish,
Strawberries and cream in a dish.
The birth of a baby, specially your own
Being away then going home.
Children's laughter at party time,
The joy of words that happily rhyme.
Squirrels playing on the grass,
A wonderful view from a mountain top pass.
Redwood trees, a thousand years old
Deep soft snow so white, so cold.
Love in the eyes of those you love
When soil is parched, rain from above.
A kitten or puppy, a newborn foal,
The joy when a son scores his first goal.
A daughter at her first ballet class
Pride and tears as veterans march past.
Whatever it takes to stir your heart
Is beauty personified right from the start.

Evelyn Mary Eagle

Assurance

God's Word declares that Christ has died to save you.
Rejoice in Him, His love to you is shown.
He cares and knows each heartache, fear and longing,
And promises you'll never be alone.
Rest thou in Him, the Risen Lord of glory;
He is thy peace, the Saviour keeps His own.
Rest thou in Him, the Risen Lord of glory;
He is thy peace, the Saviour keeps His own.

His pardon stands, the Christ who died to save you.
No one but He could for your sins atone,
His kindness know, His joy and gracious favour,
His matchless love He has toward thee shown.
Rejoice and sing for great is thy salvation,
Thou child of God, accepted as His own.
Rejoice and sing for great is thy salvation.
Thou child of God, accepted as His own.

You are His child, the Christ who lives to keep you.
His praises sing, His fullness know within.
Restored, forgiven, mercy poured upon you,
Set free from thraldom, rescued from all sin.
Ring out thy praise to Jesus King of glory,
Thou, made by faith, to thy Great Lord akin.
Ring out thy praise to Jesus King of glory,
Thou, made by faith, to thy great Lord akin.

Victor J Ensor

Forever Smiling

It was not a telephone call I heard,
neither was it a letter I received
in truth, time has passed
like one's first love
it is never forgotten.

Lying in bed, the night sky drifted past
the rain had taken breath from her dance
Gently those steps I heard
was it a rush of the wind
as she fleeted past my window?

No, said, I
I am in the land of evergreen pastures
as a newborn lamb rubs its nose to the grass
I have found my place where I can smile in the everlasting light

Yes I remember the gentleness
by which I was lifted out of my sleep,
gazing at my body as it smiled
Away I went hearing the sound of music.

From that time I have loved that call
By His blessing
I still hear those words
Come with me and you will smile forever.

Ajarn Anton Nicholas

Perfection

Perfection is an asset
Which none of us possess
Persons claim to own it
After a great redress.

Perfection - not even on ration
One single portion alone, was made
Then given to the Son of God
As human sins were displayed.

You, could never own perfection
It was never designed for you
Great men 'touched' upon it
Only one man received His due.

So, when you strive for perfection
Don't crush others in your wake
That 'being' - who is the only rightful owner
Died for all our sins and all our sakes.

Maureen Westwood O'Hara

I Am Not The Son Of God

I am not the Son of God
Whose ever God that may be
By whatever name
He is one and all the same to me
For I have sat upon the pillar
Far above the desert sands
And have been found wanting
For I am my own judge and jury
I know my sins, I know my heart
I believe in Christ
And the resurrection
I have seen good and evil
And goodness rules my heart
I commend my soul to God.

David Walford

Untitled

I have waited for my Lord on endless shores
by sea-grown beaches red and brown.
And followed with my eyes the falling sun
that left its trail of vagrant colours.

I have felt Him in the open skies
through nimbus keyholes I espied Him
and thought with little steps to reach His distance;

Certain things begin the day, the morning tea,
a prayer, a call from a friend who's left;
so these things end; but a time
shall come when there shall be no time, a state
when I shall not count the seconds, or see their end.
When these things I follow, and extend my gaze
my thought shrinks back in fear.

I shall wait for Him on time-grown shores
and follow with my steps the rising sun.

Alen Ontl

Deeper Than The Ocean

God's love is deeper than the ocean
Higher than the highest mountain
Beyond my comprehension!

My heart wants to sing praise
And give Him all the glory,
Giving thanks for what He has done,
For the sacrifice He made when
On the cross my Saviour died,
Taking the blame,
Bearing my sin and shame.

I want to spread the good news far and wide
That God who made the Earth, the sky and sea
Poured out His love, not sparing His Son
And thinks the world of me!

Cathy Mearman

Turning Point

This year has marked a turning point
In my two score years and eleven -
After all the events of the past twelve months
How can I believe in Heaven?

It started badly and just got worse
All through, right to the end
Despair has taken over
My heart will never mend.

Two friends were taken at the year's beginning
Good men - with no goodbye,
They're missed by friends and family
But carry on we must try.

Then so many more around us
In accident or by nature's hand
Both young and old, at work and play
It's hard to understand.

So many suffered by fire and flood
At home and far away,
The wars rage on, they'll never stop
The papers seem to say.

But though these things, so terrible,
Alone would break my heart,
It's the lost and stolen children
That really tear me apart.

By cruel and sadistic souls
They suffer and they cry
And no one seems to hear them,
They cannot understand why.

So many I have come to know
Their happy faces on my screen,
I read of their lives, their families' despair -
News for a moment then never seen
Nor heard of again, never to grow
Nor to fulfil their dreams.

This year has marked a turning point
In my two score years and eleven,
The only thing left I have is hope -
I pray there *is* a Heaven.

Sue Wilson

For The Loved Ones

When you look up to the sky,
And see the biggest star,
You'll know that's me looking down on you,
From a distance oh so far.

And when the night sky is clear and still,
And we seem so far apart,
Although I'm not on this Earth you know,
I'm forever in your heart.

It isn't always the things we do,
Nor in the things we say,
But you know I'll be looking down on you,
To give you hope through the passing days.

And of course you feel it unfair,
No doubt you think too soon,
But some of us have to leave early,
I guess God needs the room.

And when you're feeling lonely,
And in the moments you feel weak,
I'll be in the air that surrounds you,
The breeze that kissed your cheek.

Chantay Speed

For I Am The Lord Who Heals You
(Exodus 15:26)

Like the mighty sun
Big and round -
(I am the Lord who heads you.)
Its warmth and power -
Like my warmth and power,
Will surround you
In your hour of need.

The vast oceans
With their tremendous waves -
I am the Lord who heals you.
The salt to bathe your wounds
Is like my immense touch,
It will heal those scars
Both visible and invisible.

The playful wind
Sometimes meek and sometimes powerful -
I am the Lord who heals you.
Blowing strength into weary bones,
Breathing courage into a troubled mind.
I will never leave you -
My spirit kisses you goodnight,
When in death you will join me at my table
For I am the Lord who heals you.

Deborah Nobbs

What Will They Say?

The whole point of my life, may be hidden from me
But I have my own philosophy.
You only get out, what you're prepared to put in,
To do less than your best, must be a sin.

Our lives may be controlled by destiny or fate
But what will they say when I stand at the gate?
Will I be known for a villain or a star?
Have I been kind and considerate on par.

Who makes the decision, my God or my maker?
How will he judge me as a caretaker?
I've done my best, taking care of my life,
Brining up my children, protecting my wife.

Am I destined to be someone unknown?
Will my friends remember, have the right seeds been sown?
Will the world read my poems and understand
That I loved my life and think it grand?

What will they say when I pass away?
Will they remember me kindly for one whole day?
Is it enough that when my time arrives
My family will love me for the rest of their lives?

Can I change anything or is it too late?
Is the die cast, has God set a date?
Is love measured on a heavenly scale?
What happens to me if I falter or fail?

Brian Hurll

Angel

An angel came to me last night
Her celestial, magnificent true light
She touched my face
My soul to guide
To find the truth
Be by my side
An angel *did* come to show me right
In a shroud of heavenly soft blue light
She hopes, has faith, has love within
This gift she gives me from now herein
An angel came to me the path to show
That everlasting love
And truth
And love
Will glow
From within to those around
She whispers to me with such soft sweet sound
My guardian angel.

Sally Williams

What Is Love?

Love is patient
Love is kind
Love does not demand its own way
Love is generous
Love does not hold grudges
Love is not to cause hurt
Love is not to cause pain
Love is not to cause you to go insane
Love does not cause blame
Love is peace and does not cause war.

Annamarie Cope

Musical Dream

Music, life and soul
Beat, the flutter,
Tapping of the feet, the heart
Warmth inside, when cold outside
Happiness is a smile
Crossroads emotion
Walk away, when you want to walk close
In the distance, you still hear,
Beat, you dance
Your soul finds a way
In the emotion of the day
You sing.
Soft voices, angels of the day
They say - come
I hear - I really do
For music knows my soul

Josie Lawson

Untitled

God of spirit, God of truth
We come before You our praise to bring
As we kneel before Your throne
Our love is for You alone.

We are all Your people
Whatever colour or creed
Help us to respect each other
Give aid to those in need.

As we lift our hearts in prayer
And our voices in song
We ask that You will always be near
Someone we can lean upon.

Brenda Charles

Felicity

A bird shed a feather
without a care,
leaving it to drift
downwards in the air.

It floated until it
came to rest
in a cobweb
causing it to be well dressed.

There it fluttered
near the windowsill,
bedecked in dewdrops,
sparkling like a jewel.

When the dew evaporated
it continued its movement
bonded to the web
with great attachment.

How strange a piece of stuff
can convey such felicity
when its sheer beauty
is revealed in pure simplicity.

Suzanna Wilson

If You Can Hear Me

Lord, shine Your light gently
But, please don't blind me
For I have been waiting patiently.

I look up slowly and I see a ray
Lord, is this Your light?
I begin to pray

Lord if You can hear me
I think I'm lost
It's summer but my feet won't move
From this permafrost

Lord if You can hear me
I don't mean to complain
But it feels like the perdition is on Earth
From all this pain.

Lord if You can hear me
I really can't cope,
Every time I gain it
I lose the hope.

Lord if You can hear me
Please change my ways
Make me a better person
For my final days.

Sonya Nikolosina

Clouded

I didn't see the wayward cloud come creeping up the hill
And undulate and curve and writhe, I didn't see beyond the sill
I couldn't see the weary part of me that lay sleeping still
The troubled glance, perplexing faith, clouding out the long embrace.

I only saw the part of you, you cared to bring along
And the sadness at the part of you, that to me did not belong
I didn't see the fledgling tear, before it mustered strong
I only saw the pallid glance and then that you were gone.

The dancing dream, the daring truth, the charity eternal youth
I will look and see you yet in ferns and flowers
And keep the secrets of the crowded hours
And in the burnished vanquished strain
A cloudless essence still remain
In fracture white and dreaming skies
For after in a lost domain, softened by this gentle rain.

Ruth Alice Toy

No Sad Laments

Your loved ones will live forever
as you never really part.
God knows that you are lonely,
He will help to heal your heart.

No one can take away your pain
as your grief is always there,
but many people share your sorrow
and God will always care.

The road may be long and lonely
but you do not walk alone,
if you let God walk beside you
as you go into the unknown.

You hold on to your memories
like a beautiful love song,
your grief will never grow old
as it if forever young.

Doreen Hampshire

Will We Ever Learn?

The most precious gift God gave to me
He gave me life and gave it free.
He gave me senses, six in all,
He gave sights and sounds that would enthral.
The flash of an iridescent butterfly,
The songbird trilling way up high,
Flowers and bushes everywhere
And green, green grasses waving in the air.
Flowing rivers, babbling brooks,
Awesome sights where're one looks.
To see such sights in every day
Makes life a joy in every way.
Sometimes man tends these sights so well
Tho' at other times he makes them hell,
Man cares for money in the bank
So when you see a mess you'll know who to thank.

Rosie Hues

His Love is . . .

His love is strong, faithful and true
It will always be there for you.
His love is a barrier, always taking care
When life is too much for you to bear.
His love is a house and also a home
That will go with you wherever you roam.
His love is like a soothing breeze
To cool a summer's day
His love is like a winding lane
To follow when you lose your way.
His love is never ending
That will go on into eternity
His love is for His children
That means you and me.

Shirley Sewell

Begging Letters

Through my letterbox I hear their cry, folded tight
inside envelopes. The screams of African famine,
the fly attack children that are starving and dying,.
The torn hearts of those who care, and their final pledge that
any donation, however small, would feed a whole family today.
Yet in the vastness of Africa's variable and giant continent,
any amount is but a drop in an ocean of human suffering,
a bottomless abyss from drought, famine and war,
that together we must all help to breach, and for humanity's
                                                         sake reach.

Asia's children that live in dirty infested gutters,
know no home other than the paving streets,
through their eyes of bewilderment, innocents, shout and plead
for food to eat and a roof over their head to sleep.
Their tears and cries, touch our well-fed heart,
not answering our neighbour's plight would be wrong,
as one once said, 'Suffer little children unto Me, as theirs is the
                                                Kingdom of Heaven.'
It is by helping these street and homeless children that we live
the message Jesus taught, and our reward is that which cannot
                                                      be bought, love.

South America and the Philippines is another cry
where their faith is as strong, as their need for food,
the heartache of each and every individual child
whose needs are greater than the lease.
Leaves one asking the age old question,
how can we, with much, just look and stand aside
not weep and feel for those poor children in need
without seeing Jesus face and our own helplessness
at the dying of a single child, not practice
the best parable of the Good Samaritan, stop and give money aid.

In truth, not only in the Third World does the cry of the poor go unheard,
as beneath the veneer of our cities industrial wealth,
lives a world unspoken of, people living half dead.
Without much notice they are sadly trodden upon
their outstretched hands for crumbs to live,
left empty, on seeing them, we ignore them and hurry quickly by
in our rush to nowhere we become socially blind.
Nimble drones in an industrial driven beehive
to treat our fellow human beings is a begging crime.

Philip Anthony McDonnell

My Own Angel

Heaven was falling to the ground
Waves of sparkly angels no sound
Give me a sign if the dawn is in sight
I'm alone in the darkness and long is the night

An angel robed in spotless white
Bends over to kiss the sleeping night
She spreads her wings and starts to fly
A breeze comes and the warm night begins to die

Wake up my angel, please say my name
My soul is on fire and I can't feel the flame
Visions are dancing across a blank screen
Tell me angel, nightmares, is it a bad dream?

Your angel's hair sways as you turn your cheek
Reflecting the stars all gentle and meek
A tear trickles down your face which starts anew
That covers the garden with morning dew.

You said hello to a whole new day
And look forward to the night to come your way
Guardian angel whose patience is gentle and kind
Bring me sweet comfort and joyous peace of mind.

Victorine Lejeune-Stubbs

Get Through

Outcome afar, it's near to the end,
All pressures around you
With a need to befriend.
Accomplish between you, a right to be firm,
At strong arms together,
And no one to squirm.
Each man to the last
In ages lifespan
We'll achieve what we've set out
As our own mortal plan.
Having each to consider
A well thought out phrase
That will stand to our stead
 But survive all your days.
Some may be anxious, an hour to debate,
All reasons of hazard
From the time we came late.
Lots more discussions, all questions ask why
When it comes to the crunch time
Now the cause will apply.
We've thought it, fought it,
Lived the life,
That brought us through the anguished strife
Will we each do our part
That comes from the heart
And decide in the long run
To put horse before cart.

Hugh Campbell

Beyond The Cross

I share her open-eyed embrace
of sense that man is but a blink
of eye in cosmic scene of play
of births and deaths.

I share her praise of beauties seen
in nature's rich display, from bug
that's viewed with microscope to spread
of Milky Way.

I'm pleased to know, beyond her grief,
her sense of awe survives her act
of ditching God whose heartless ways
fanatics preach.

She's right to bin pernicious lies
that some employ to wrap the truth,
concealed beneath accretion's crust,
but not the gold.

I just regret her loss of faith
in God of love conferring sense
of purpose on our lives with call
to walk with Christ.

Beyond His cross and Easter's joy
we're offered grace that rescues us
from selfish drives of creeping
things from which we came.

Henry Disney

If My World Was A Canvas

If my world was a canvas
All stark and white without restraint,
I would just let me brush alight.
Without any care
Splash here, daub there,
Using a plethora of strokes
Attack that canvas bare.
I would paint my world
In a vibrant hue
With slash oranges,
Candy reds
And delphinium blue.
Not sparing a second
To stop and think,
Uncaring if I tainted
Any shape or form.
Total nonconformity
That's the style of life,
I would paint just for me
Just let my artistic soul run free.
And when I am eventually done
I think there would not be anyone
Who would understand
My life in a multicoloured wonderland.

Michael Campbell

Untitled

Oh little child, oh precious one
I love you dear, my infant son
And in my heart I know you read
The love that swells and does not heed
The pain I'll undergo.

For you are gift beyond desire
And, though my son, you are my sire.
And when I clasp you to my breast
My soul is bowed in worship, blessed
Must be your name.

And though in days, which loom ahead,
A cross is borne and blood is shed,
I see your face and ends the pain
And in my heart loves comes again
For you, my own.

And it will be the same for all
Who find this child and heed his call,
For deepest sorrow will turn to joy
And pain seem sweet, my darling boy
When they see your face.

Petya Christie

Omar's Thoughts

When young I heard every argument
That teachers and preachers did present.
But now I see that they were passing on
Fallacies from down the ages and anon.

Mankind strives to unearth the secret scheme
But fails to find it behind some hidden screen.
He catches a glimpse maybe, but not for long,
It escapes his grasp like the blackbird's song.

I'm forever searching for answers of my own
Conflicting thoughts are clouding every dawn.
For thousands of years, Mankind has tried
To unearth those truths, but they still hide.

I've formed many ideas but they don't last
In a brief spell of time they soon have passed.
Atoms of truth have flashed through my brain
But quickly vanished and not returned again.

You would have thought that in all the years
Just one or two people would return as seers.
Will the questions we ask, ever be solved
Or is there simply nothing to be resolved?

Prepare well, in the days that you have left,
Then settle quietly before going to your rest.
Your final thoughts should leave you calm
In the certain truth that you did no harm.

I'll stop searching and share bread and wine
With a true love held close, beneath the vine.
Whispering leaves make a sensuous sound,
When nature's perfect paradise is all around.

John Troughton

Unwanted Advice

Are you often told which way to go?
You're travelling through life too fast, too slow,
And don't do that, do this instead,
Conflicting views spin round your head.

'We're doing this for your own good'
'Do go there, you know you should.'
'Don't take that advice, mine is better,
You really shouldn't buy that sweater.'

Are you thinking of going to the shops today,
'Seriously?' I hear one say.
Take time to relax, you'll enjoy it more
To rush around shops would be a chore.

Then another says, 'Don't sit back
Get out, look around, don't be so slack.'
Another chips in, 'No, just you wait,
Why don't you sit and contemplate?'

'Don't give Tom that much, a card will do'
I hold my breath my face turning blue.
They care for me, they say with a grin
I am sick and sick of giving in.

No more for me conflicting views
For in the end, it's me who'll choose.
After bombarding me with worthless chatter
It's what I think that will really matter.

Barbara Lambie

Treasures Of Friendship

To find a heart as warm as your own
Reaching out an invitation into your home.
Everlasting memories together we do share
Always knowing that you will be there.
Silent tears I may cry
Under the stars of the southern sky
Remembering times now gone by
Enduring - you are a dear friend of mine
Stories we tell that bring a smile.

Of times, of secrets that are never to be told
Friendship is a gift that can never be bought or sold.

For in life, it is something you hold ever so dear
Remembering the moments when you were near.
Inspiring my mind in the saddest of times
Endless love that you gave without a sigh.
Never leaving me to stand alone
Day by day, your friendship you have always shown.
Sharing together with a bond now strong
Holding close our friendship all life long.
In the time to come and pass on by
Promises we made to last all our life.

Susan Russell-Smith

Entertaining Angels

When travelling on every day journeys
Meeting empathetic strangers
Listening to life's glimpse of our
Personal journey so far
Feeling the way forward
We are gladdened by the encounter
We may never know
When we are entertaining angels.

Brian Tallowin

Coming To Terms

When your heart is heavy and life seems bare
You feel this emotion because you care.
Life seems bleak and your soul is sad
Your very existence, express bad so bad.
Do not despair, this will not last
Just think of the future don't dwell on the past.
What has gone is just beyond the shade
Never forgotten, not too far away.
Memories give comfort and gladden the heart
Life never dies, you're just moments apart.
There will always be a beginning but never an end
For you and your family and also your friends.

Mary E Gill

Stories

From two words, 'I'm fine -
which hide much -
to thousands of words printed down.

Language bustling in our heads,
like a phone conversation
that travels the globe with no rest.

Stifled secrets are stories untold,
which hurt those who are old,
the young who still have to grow.

Parables are stories the hearers
of Jesus understood, these
spiritual telescopes point ahead.

Stories drawn into dance
painted on stones,
shown in stained glass, or
by veins on the back of a hand,
our feet print the receding sand.

Naomi Lange

The Embryo (Meant To Be)

I am given an existence
To elevate, even procreate
Another fish in the sea
I am meant to be
I can stretch, I can feel
Not ready yet to breathe
I can hear, I can see
I am as safe as I am meant to be
A body, even a soul
I am part of life's goal
I have tears to cry, words to heal
Love to give for others to feel
There is pain to endure
Through a belief instilled
Times to feel steady again
After feeling ill
There is time for food
Time for thought
Chances to build
Chances to be taught
Chances to teach others
All I can learn
Chances to reach out
Many stones to turn
I'll have stories to tell
Tales to hear
I'll have joy to give
And time to control fear
I have laughter to absorb
Night and days to travel
To stare at the stars with awe
Life is awesome
But there is a fate
Worst than being deported
My dreams all deserted
The day I was aborted

I was given chances
To add to Man's advances
Another fish in the sea
But someone else decided
My life was not meant to be.

Mike Hynde

Don't Let Me Die

My eyes won't stay open Lord
please don't let me die
in this foreign land
with no one by my side.
I have tried to fight well
and look after all my mates
but now I'm being called
to Your pearly gates.
The mud is so cold
and the night is dark
I'm not really afraid
but the place is so stark.
I can see all my family,
my babies and wife
crying and wailing
for my poor lost life.
I come to Your keeping,
my life in your hands
Praying this war ends soon
and men leave this war torn land.

Ann Morgan

The Holy Rap

Lord give me a sign
I really need to talk to You Lord
since the last time we talked
the walk has been hard.

Now I know you haven't left me
but I feel like I'm alone
I'm a big boy now
but I'm still not grown.

I'm still going through it
the pain and the hurt
soaking up my troubles
like the rain in the dirt.

I know I could stop the rain
with just a mention of my Saviour's name,
the name of Jesus

Devil I rebuke you for what I go through
and trying to make me do what I used to do.

All that stops right here -
as long as the Lord's in my life I'll have no fear.
I'll know no pain
from the light to the dark
I'll show no shame
say it straight from the heart,
'cause right from the start you held me down.

So go to pester someone else now
'cause the Lord's given me a sign
show me what I got to do
to get closer to you
'cause I'll go through whatever You want me to.

Just let me know what to do
help me and help my mind
just like You helped
Jesus cure the blind.
Amen.

Steven Williams

Down The Line

Life is like a book
each chapter, starting at the birth.
Full of ups and downs, twists and turns
and for what it's worth.
All the sadness and the sorrow mixed
with the happiness and joy.
Throughout each chapter it differs
for each girl and boy.
Few have a full and joyful life
with no downs at all.
And even in the saddest life
the sun will often fall.
For we all have our moments
I thank God for all of mine
Because out of the bleakest cloud
the sun would often shine.
And now as years are passing
faster that before.
I have little time to squander
so much to do and more.
Thank God for my blessings and the
hard times that made me strong.
And for all my achievements
although the road was long.
There are so many chapters
in this my lifetime book,
with ups and downs like everyone
and so much contentment now everywhere I look.

Irene Keeling

Life Rhythms

Cyclic intersections sing
in harmony, when tender
raindrops create hushed
melodies, gently drumming
against the windowsill.

Natural instincts grow
with time, strengthened
day by day as a tiny heart
sets the loving tone, framing
future moments with hope.

Rhythmic collaborations make
and break, the cycles of life
continuing invisibly in echoes
carried forward to the present,
in sounds only the soul can hear.

Caroline Skanne

The End

The end of the world as we know it
Our planet is in dire decline
Earth is ready to take a bow
As she prepares to speak her last lines.
An epic ending in the theatre of life
On the stage of civilisation
Lights are ready to fade to black
Over every nation.
Global catastrophe
The final applause
Unless we act
And fight a good cause.
The world is taking a hammering
From humans and their fumes
It's time to start making a difference
The last act looms
Curtains will soon close.

Donna Salisbury

Finding Faith

F aith is the etching of the soul the
A ssured forgiveness to make whole an
I nspired need to reach a goal that
T rusting guidance in destined role,
H eeding that never exacts toll.

H D Hensman

God's Rainbow

When I'm down I'm blue,
When I'm sick I'm yellow,
When I'm jealous I am green,
When I'm well I'm rosy,
When I'm angry I'm purple,
When I'm suicidal I am black.
God shines into the darkness;
All of the colours mingle;
In the white light
God turns darkness into beauty,
Takes each of my moods,
Melds it with His
Till all I know is His love
Surrounding me,
Holding me,
Filling me,
Teaching me,
Encouraging me
Till all I have is His and He is mine.
God of the rainbow
God of the free
God of all
And God of me.

Sue Reilly

Step By Step

Not knowing is the hardest part,
Waiting anxiously for an answer is even harder.
Left to the imagination the mind drifts to the unknown.
A secret place where all your thoughts are stored,
Some good and some bad.
To regain a balance you not only accept but surrender
To the unpredictability of life taking one step at a time.

Ise Obomhense

Psalm

Oh Lord my God
Who will comfort me
If not You?
Who shall I turn to
If not You?
If You do not come to my aid
What shall become of me?

For it is in You only I trust
It is only You I rely on
Therefore if You leave me
Who shall I lean on?
To whom shall I turn to?
For evil is before me
And weak as I am
I cannot overcome it.

Come to my rescue
Oh Lord and prove
Your Word to me
Let the world know and believe
That You love me
And You will never leave me alone.

Debra Ayis

Don't Give In

The spirit within says you will win
If you keep going and don't give in.
Though at times things may seem grim
Just keep trying and never give in.

Set your mind on a certain goal
Although you feel you're stuck in a hole.
Make a fresh start and try again
Though your hopes are starting to wane.

Don't sit and ponder and let your mind wander
Tell yourself you're going to win
Listen to that little voice
Of the spirit within.

Violetta Jean Ferguson

Silence

Precious is silence;
A gift from Heaven.
In this noisy world
A moment to treasure.
No roaring of wind
In the chimney.
No thundering wheels of traffic;
No screech of changing gear.
No loud voices on television
Often in angry mood.
They are hidden away
In their box enclosure
So the room
Is full of my thoughts
And a deep peace
Surrounds me wholly,
And wraps me in joy
Builds up inner strength;
Helps me carry on
Through life's difficult moments.

Mary Johnson-Riley

So To Believe

Once there was a farmer, who believed not in God's plan
That the Son would come to Earth, to take the form of mortal man!
He shrugged off this notion, as too preposterous in extreme,
Never would he have the faith to accept this impossible scheme.
The winter now had come; the winds so bitter did blow,
And with it came a blizzard, covering the fields with snow.
A flock of geese exhausted, landed shelter needing to seek,
But so icy was the cold, each moment they grew more weak.
The farmer was truly concerned, lighting up he warmed his barn,
He tried to entice the geese, to prevent them from coming to harm.
But the birds evaded his efforts, escaping from the grasp of his hand,
He racked his brain for ways, to make them understand.
A glimmer of an idea struck him, he'd try to act like a goose,
Then maybe they'd follow his footsteps and not perish by running loose.
Suddenly comprehension, this was the good Lord's way!
Yes the Christ *had* come to Earth, in the form of man *did* stay!
Another soul enlightened, falling on his knees to pray!
Oh this wondrous gift is Jesus, our Saviour this very day!

Cecilia Jane Skudder

Why?

Why are we tearing this world apart?
Is it too much trouble, to even ask?
Why not try peace?

Why are we set on killing each other
Country against country, brother against brother?
Why not try peace?

Why the aggression, no love or forgiving
It's not just the wars, it's everyday living.
Why not try peace

Why ruin the world, it's big enough to share?
We'll soon be too old, too tired, to care
Why not try peace?

Patricia Lay

Breaking Point

What is the point?
There is none really.

The constant grind wears me down
and repetitive chores bore me.
Stress arrives through the letterbox,
cyberspace and the telephone
daily.

Nerves are stretched taut.
Elongated
almost to breaking point.

And yet . . . and yet . . .

I have invested too much to let go;
to snap.

Positive thoughts, bracing walks
a sense of perspective regained.
Breaking point recedes
beyond a sunlit horizon.

Brenda Artingstall

The Loving Heart

Love weaves its heart in threads so fine,
so fine that only love could know
what grace the infinite bestows
upon all those
whose heart doth show
and care enough
to freely give in dedication unto need, and
in its giving
does commit, without thought to prejudice or creed,
to serve,
with willing heart,
each loving deed.

Diana Mudd

Understanding

Why do folks hold grudges
And cause each other pain?
Why can't they be forgiving,
What have they got to gain?
Their lives would be more pleasant
If they turned the other cheek,
People would admire them more
And not think of them as weak.
This world has many troubles
That it holds for us in store,
So where is the advantage
In seeking out some more?
Why can't we learn the lesson
That history has taught?
So many wars have started
Over things that mattered not.
So if you really feel annoyed
By something someone said
Just treat the matter calmly
Try not to lose the head!
You'll find that you feel better
And won't lose so much sleep
If you are forgiving
And you your temper keep.
So step out into the future
Let troubles pass you by
Be lots more understanding
You know you can if you just try.

Ian Russell

A Child Of God

It is up to you and me friend
To every day impart
To our brothers and our sisters
A message from the heart.

For each day be thankful
For every living thing
See all that is around you
See the beauty that He brings.

When your heart is full of sorrow
And your load too hard to bear
Embrace a newborn baby
Hold it gently in your care.

Feel the birth that is around you
In the flowers and the fields
Go out into the woodlands
And see the life it yields.

Look at the dawning of each spring
How it lifts the spirits high
And feel your God around you
As you gaze upon the sky.

As you journey through this life friend
Upon there seas and on the land
Be glad you are a child of God
A soul made by His hand.

Elizabeth Slater Hale

Light

Shafts of light radiate from above,
Filtering through the canopy of the native trees
Down on to the forest floor,
Spotlighting the ferns and wild flowers.
Silently deer are grazing upon the sparse grasses,
And cock pheasants echo their rasping calls to others,
From the outer boundaries of fields and hedges.

The tall trees are like wooden pillars,
A natural cathedral of light,
And in the beauty and the peacefulness of this place
God's presence is found.

The ancient cathedral is bathed in rainbows,
As sunlight shines through leaded glass windows
Down on to the old stone floor.
People silently pray to their heavenly Father
As lit candles radiate light in dark corners,
Reminding us that Jesus is the Light of the World.

Linda Knight

Depends On How One Looks At Things

I could tell you about the rain
The wetness, the cold lancing sheets
splitting the ear and thundering on the tin roof.
But I won't.

I'll tell you about the pool,
the silver shrouded fish,
the wet ferns heavily bent
and the white mist rising.

I could sit all day and stare with delight
at the beauty created here,
this mystery, from whence it has come,
in the aftermath of the storm in the night.

Pearl Foy

Happy Feelings

When I'm feeling low and sad
I think of things that make me glad.
Birds singing in the trees
The buzzing on flowers of the bees.
Children playing on the swings
And doing lots of other things.
Flowers in gardens of every hue
Grass early morning glistening with dew.
A newborn baby looking sweet
The taste of strawberries for a treat.
Having chocolate when in the bath
Getting messy, but what a laugh.
A walk in the park on a lovely day
Smelling the scent of new mown hay.
A lovely song played on the air
Reading a book in a favourite chair.
Seeing children dressing up
Their joy when given another new pup.
Recalling these things makes me glad
Then I am no longer low or sad.

Diana Daley

Thou Art God

Thou art my Saviour this very day,
Thou are the Light, the Truth, the Way,
Through life, Thou art my love.
Keep me from ill, Thou art my Lord and with me still,
Thou art the calling of the poor,
Thou art the stranger at the door.
Thou art the guest who waits inside
Thou art the door that's open wide
Thou art the heart's eternal spark,
Thou art the light that shines in dark,
Thou art the place to hide form harm,
Thou art the peace, joy of all things calm,
Thou art the Way the Truth, the Life.

Imogene Lindo

Aging Thoughts

When I was young, I could run and walk
Now that I am older, I just sit and talk.
When I was young, my life was lots of fun and games
Now that I am older, I suffer a few aches and pains.
When I was young, I had ambitions galore
Now that I am older, I do not seek them anymore.
When I was young, on my head I grew a mop of hair
Now that I am older, alas, it is no longer there.
When I was young, my teeth were white and gleamed
Now that I am older, at night they are in a glass to clean.
When I was young, I had too little time to spare
Now that I am older, I have lots of time to share.
When I was young, my mind was quick and sharp
Now that I am older, I find it has lost its spark.
When I was young I lived through troubles and strife
Now that I am older, I am world wise and enjoying the time of my life.

Leonard Butler

Yesterday's Dreams

Yesterday's dreams of today were never clear.
Now that today is here, they've turned quite grey.
There's too much inbetween to keep our focus,
events that choke us, blur the swirling scene
quite out of kilter. Needs must realign
our dreams and redefine what we can filter
from the best morass. Of what remains,
any salvaged gains that come to pass,
looked at in retrospect, must seem a bonus,
the ensuing onus of their use for us to dissect,
assess how much was truer and how much not.
There's one part of the plot we know for sure:
however diffuse the schemes the gods may feed us,
whatever roads they lead us are yesterday's dreams.

Adrian Brett

Your New Home

May you find peace in your new home,
happiness in abundance,
wealth, health and strength,
joy beyond measure, days full of pleasure.
May you hear birds
chirping sweetly through
the rustling leaves
of the trees that adorn
your pretty garden.
May only loving footsteps
walk your path and
sit by your hearth, to
engage in friendly banter.
May you be blessed with
many blessings, in your new home.

Penny Kirby

Hope

God is our hope
If we let Him be
With hope in our hearts
We will always be free.

God is our hope
Without it we're lost
A gift to cling onto
And keep at all cost.

God is our hope
The rock of our life
Our light in the dark
Hope overcomes strife.

God is our hope
On Him we depend
He knows what's best
His hope has no end.

Jackie Graham

Required Of Life

Stated clear in a lengthy scroll of old
Is shown how to live upon the land
It was found in old St Paul's church that told
I wrote it down clear to understand.
Go undisturbed among the noise and haste
And let silence be your peace of mind
Be on good terms throughout the human race
So speak quiet and clear throughout Mankind.

Hear others too, for they must have their say
Although dull and ignorant they may be
Avoid a person's loud aggressive way
They are a vexation your spirit flees
Compare not thyself to many others
For bitter, vain, this you may become
Enjoy achievements, your plans you cover
Take more interest in your career if you have one.

Exercise caution in business affairs
For the world is full of trickery
For there's no one else in the world that cares
This could be your downfall of misery
People strive for high potential ideas
Do not pretend false love and friendship
Distress not thyself with image appears
Strengthen your spirit for such hardship.

Gracefully surrender the things of youth
Take all your misfortunes as they come
And utter only that, which is the truth
Life is like a victory that is won
Discipline, but be gentle with yourself
You are a child of the universe
For many fears are born, through nothing else
But fatigue, loneliness and much thirst.

In the noisy confusion of one's life
You have a right in this world to live
Take kindly to advise that's given rife
Strive to be happy, help and to give
For the world is so very beautiful
So keep peace with your world and with God
And enjoy life when it is so plentiful
Take care with every step you have trod.

Margaret Burtenshaw-Haines

I Walked The Rugged Pathway

I walked the rugged pathway
And the rocks did hurt My feet
The cross I bore was heavy
And I'd no shade from the heat.

Some people there did mock Me
While some others turned away
Some people tried to help me then
But they were kept at bay.

The journey there was very long
And I became so weak
Yet I was kicked and spat upon
But turned the other cheek.

They tied Me to that wooden cross
Then nailed My hands and feet
A crown of thorns they gave Me
And accused Me of deceit.

And so they raised Me to the sky
And black clouds hid the sun
And I screamed, 'It is finished'
For my work on Earth was done.

Andrew Blakemore

Mary's Song

I cannot believe
That He's so small
I feel I might crush His tiny finger
In my girlish palm,

He's, so powerless
That if I do not attend to His infant cries
I will cause Him such distress
My heart would break

He's so simple,
That the touch of my hand comforts Him
And the brush of my cheek
Causes His small mouth to laugh

Is He
Whose vastness filled the heavens
Whose power caused this universe to be
And whose heart and will
Gave up the bliss of paradise
The company of angels
Of His Father - Lord himself -
To endure
An agony of death
For me,

That I whose arms rejoiced
To cradle His tiny form
Smeared with birth blood
Must years on
Cradle in my arms
The adult body of a son
Whose blood gushed forth in death
That I might be free
That we
Might for all time be free.

Karen Wood

Freedom

My dreams, ambitions, heart's desire
Passions stilled, no blazing fire.
I could not fly beyond waxing moon
But must dance to others tune.
Relationships which early bloomed
Were soon to wither and were doomed.
Because of fears repressed in me
I could not live, I was not free.
To be myself, my passions show
With fresh new love's shining glow.
The years passed by, life's waning moon
And still I danced to others tune.
Relationships formed, though they were few
Still never flourished, never grew.
I realised and in my sadness found
Those early fears, they still bound.
I wept, I prayed, in despair so deep
I even longed for eternal sleep.
I saw my life's fast waning moon
Yet still I danced to others tune.
But suddenly in later years
My loving Father eased my fears.
I saw as through another's eyes
I could reach up, reach for the skies.
I could dance to my own tune
By light of shining bright full moon.
This chance my God He gave to me
New paths to follow, to set me free.
Occasionally I still have found
I'm still by former fears bound
But I'm encouraged God's image to show
Reflected in new moon's radiant glow
His gifts, emotions, insight - they're me
Created in His image - to be free.

Brenda Hughes

Easter 2008

This year Easter is early.
This year the egg comes before the fish.
Church bells jingle jangle merrily
And return from Rome to grant every child's wish.
Hidden in the garden in each nook and cranny
Are the creations of the chocolatier.
Many an Easter egg, lamb and bunny
Beribboned and in foil shine like the jewels of Guinevere.
Listen while the fairies tinkle the bluebells.
Hearken while pixies blow daffodil trumpets.
Pearls of laugher echo like waves in cockleshells.
Sticky buds of horse chestnut glisten with droplets.
Despite his icy fingers and cloak of darkness
Samhain's season has bright berries and cones of fir and pine.
Now as we welcome Imboic with his warmer caress
Catkins scatter pollen like gold dust in sunshine.

This year but eight days separate
Easter and April Fools' Day.
Dare to celebrate New Year on the wrong date
Or like a foolish fish fail to get away
Then you'll become a poisson d'avril
With a paper fish stuck on your back.
So whether you're in Limoges or Lille
Watch out when the sun leaves Pisces in the zodiac.

But life is not all fun and games
Though few feel the pain of Good Friday.
Man still murders and maims.
It is time for fair play
In anticipation
Or our resurrection.

Vivienne Brocklehurst

Sunday School And The Outing!

Count your blessings, we sang,
As her nimble fingers ran across the old piano keys.
The yearly scripture exams behind us we await the Whitsun service.
Our anniversary, our recitations learned
And musical duets for those with voices
To entertain the village, what a good job Ivy makes of those children!
At last the prizes given and the certificates
The greatest prize a bible, inscribed with her small neat hand.

Jesus wanted us for his sunbeams, we were willing
Waiting for the bull-nosed coach to take us off to Haying Island
Littlehampton or Margate.
She in a crisp shirtwaister and neat sandals, a new hat for the outing,
We clutching new tin buckets and spades,
Thoughts of frothy, once a year candyfloss, fish and chips for tea
Our mothers for once relaxing
Watching the endless journeys with buckets of salty water
                                        for our moats.

We were all so happy, the sun always shining
Even the journey home, with an occasional try at 'Ten Green Bottles'
Was quiet now and drowsy,
Our only discomfort the dusty moquette seats against our sunburn
We were safe in our little world with ivy.
Even now through cuttings with high chalk sides I still see her
'This is the sort of place the Good Samaritan helped that poor man'
She said, leaving a picture for evermore imprinted in our minds.

Mary Anne Clock

Redeemer Of My Soul

Oh my God how can I think of thee?
Redeemer of my soul
It lifts my heart to think how great You are
Sometimes when in despair I stumble
You take my hand and lead me to another day.

Oh Lord, be beside me when I stumble
And take me to another day
For I am weak but strong with You beside me
So be there with me when I stray.

So dear Lord of all creation
To Thy feet our tributes bring
I have no wealth or diamonds
To bequeath to You my king.

Oh Lord, be beside me when I stumble
And take me to another day
For I am weak but strong with You beside me
So be there with me when I stray.

But thou who knows my heart
Is Yours for ever and a day
Will accept the love I bring You
And be beside me all the way.

Oh Lord be beside me when I stumble
And take me to another day
For I am weak but strong with You beside me
So be there with me when I stray.

Joan May Wills

Treasures Of The Heart

An angel's whisper of love
helped me again today.
Yesterday's visions are fading
only photographs remain.
The treasures in my heart
give me the strength to live.
As I face life's hardships
each and every day.
Love within a family
I believe is beyond any wealth.
No money will ever buy
the treasures of my heart.
True friends never ask you
to live their impossible dreams.
Their smiles and friendship
are treasures of the heart.
An angel's whisper of love
helped me again today.
Yesterday's visions are fading
only photographs remain.
A treasure of my heart
is the loving memory of you.
Being alone can be daunting
within life's fast lane.
You are a treasure of my heart
and you wait for me in Heaven.
Until my hour is ever silent
I'll be missing you.

Russell Mortimer

The Suffering Saviour

The soldiers must have wondered at
The crushing stark finality
Of actions sanctioned by the law;
Their minds foreshadowed consequences,
But consciences might be betrayed,
As that unyielding, bloodstained man
Stretched helpless on the length of wood,
Was likewise cruelly betrayed.

No recompense for what they did,
Except for loud applause at each
And every hammer blow that struck
The nails, to pin the feet and hands
Onto the rough-hewn timbered cross.
The sounds disturbed the zephyred air;
So shocked the mind and gripped the soul,
Yet nothing purged the hurt, the shame,
The numbing of the human spirit.

The cross was hauled up into place.
His body sagged, the pain increased:
He pleaded for release with God
To end the madness of it all.
His voice took wing, soared up through space
Towards the night's cathedral vault,
Ablaze with starry chandeliers.
His message, thus conducted on
Through time to distant galaxies,
Brought meaning to a universe,
In so much need of love and peace.

So God was thus regenerated,
When Jesus' spirit left its host.

Raymond W Seaton

Far From The City

Far from the city
Pained arms outstretched
In self giving and
Infinite gathering
You await a lost traveller
On the path of the forsaken, one
Alone in the valley of the shadow.

Always you journeyed softly
Entering inner tumult
Ministering Your gift
Of healing light.
Now, frail and broken
As a leaf in autumn
You touch secret places of
The heart with peace from forgiveness.

'Forgive them, they know
Not what they do.'
Not mere words but
Vibrations from a longing heart
Felt by the lost and
Frightened child who is humanity.
Truly I thirst for You longing to
Receive You into the true divine abiding

I know too well that
It need not be like this.
Away from divided society
Also from divided outward
Religion then, as now
You are shepherding, knocking
On closed doors seeking
To love and gather in peace.

George Coombs

He Is Risen!

He is risen!
Joyful news that Easter brings
To dispel the gloom and sadness
From hearts oppressed by many things,
For its message brings release -
Love divine's great masterpiece.

For Christ, the Saviour, lives today
To be our friend, companion, guide
Along the route of life's untrodden pathway
Where in Him we can securely abide,
Trusting in His love and grace
And feel the comfort of His warm embrace.

For the rich promise of His blessings
Through the Cross are meant for all
To enhance their lives with fragrance -
The fragrance of Christ's love to so enthral
Other lives, which sense His presence
And feel His sweet compelling influence.

Stanley Birch

My Easter Wish

Greetings as Easter is here once again
It's a time to be with family and friends.
Some have had Lent as a time to abstain,
Pray, doing good deeds or making amends.
Easter eggs and chocolates, for me and you,
Easter bunnies and bonnets are such fun,
With spring in the air, it's a world anew:
For some, it's home, others fly to the sun.
For Christians good Friday's a solemn day,
Passover's begun for Jews, solemn too
And Friday is also Mohammed's birthday;
All in one spirit - with Buddhists and Hindu.
Let God not weep at this poignant time
Let man join together with prayers sublime.

Mary May Robertson

Rock

You are the rock
On which I stand
When I follow in Your footsteps
You hold my hand.

When I am down
You lift me up
When I was full of sin
You died for me.

I learn from Your teachings
As you give me all Your knowledge
You are the light in my darkest place
You were the life when I was dead.

You showed me the way
When I was lost
When I was in need
You answered my prayer.

Chris T Tanithe

The Atonement

Indebted to Him above
He who gives us endless love
He laid down His life for us
He paid for all ours sins
He sacrificed Himself for us
To show to us His eternal love
His act of grace redeemed us all
Where'on, if men build
They cannot fall.
He broke the bands of death
That bound us all.

Carole Ann Hort

Easter At St Saviours On The Cliff

We love St Saviours on the Cliff
When, as if theatre makes symbolic shrove real
We're made to feel like the Lord's there.
And that's best at Easter time, isn't it?
High geographically, high church as well,
Swelling the organ as clergy emerge.
Priests in procession with choir arriving
Glide for Christ's sake down the aisle and,
Swinging the incense immensely proceed
To amplify Jesus' need nailed to a tree.
There's agony who can't feel deep scale?
Inhale the vapour and listen to ringing.
BC made AD, He, not faking death, dares prepare to rise.
Not dodge God's objective
The altar's stripped
We scatter.

Kenneth Lane

Love - Disposed

The brutal sounds of violence done
In answer to the daily run
From what despair has conscience fled
Where once the touch of loving led?
When pain and need makes its mark
Where is the warm and loving heart?
So much abandoned, swept aside,
No one looked at the child who cried
No one noticed his terrified eyes
As resentments exchanged harsh replies.
Ending as usual, ignoring pleas
In another drunken spree
Giving in to rage without thought or care
For the fear and suffering it left there.
Where once the touch of loving led
From what despair has conscience fled.

Colleen Biggins

Mary's Easter Song Of Joy!

Out of the garden, Mary ran with joy
With exhilaration and with conviction
Out of the garden, Mary ran with elation
To return to the disciples, still on their beds
Peter, Andrew, James and John
Mary the mother and the other women too.

Out of the garden as the rising sun
Disclosed its miracle, Mary ran
With speed, wonder and jubilation
Finding her Lord on Easter morn
Out of the garden as the rising sun
Put forth its rays
Finding her Lord on Easter morn.

Margaret Bennett

God Of Hope

Born of a radiant dream
Dead on Good Friday
You pierce with your risen light
Our world still split by evil and sin.
Only You were born of perfect love
To save our irrelevant Fridays
From the mocking eyes of despair.
Unable to descend into your humility
We do not nurture
Your flesh, diminished
By dozens of self-inflicted ills.

With Your healing power, shed yet again
The spirit of love You poured out
To the uttermost in Good Friday death
And glorious resurrection.

Angela Cutrale Matheson

Easter's Fruition

'You are from dust, to dust you will return';
That was the curse that God cast on Adam,
The day he disobeyed His commandment
And ate the fruit from Tree of Knowledge, banned.

The reign o'er Earth, God entrusted to him,
Adam through sin surrendered to Satan;
Satan became the ruler of this Earth;
Ever since, death has reigned over mankind.

But the same day, God promised deliverance,
That serpent's head be crushed by woman's seed
Which was fulfilled when Jesus through His death
Destroyed the Devil that had power of death.

Thus Christ died for men's sins, but conquered death
When on the third day He rose up from the dead,
That Man condemned to death through Adam's sin
Be made alive, to walk in newness of life.

He who hears Jesus' words, believes on Him,
Reckons himself to be dead unto sin,
But alive unto God through Jesus Christ;
His soul shifts from death to eternal life.

Thus Easter splits history into two;
Ends era of bondage to sin and curse,
Begins an epoch of deliverance
From Satan's reign of curse o'er Earth.

When Jesus comes again with trumpets' sound
And mortals put on immortality
Death will be then swallowed in victory.
That will be Easter's triumphant fruition.

Nithie Victor

He Was God's Son

Ye tribune by yon high milestone
Thine ear if thou's dare
Speak the tongue which be my own -
Thy men be standing here
On both sides thy evil charge
Conscripts all in line
Officers and troops at large
Far beyond the Rhine
Enter thee my quarters here
Through the earth-staked wall
Thy followers can rest down there
Room enough for all

So plaintiff thou - that howling mob
That thou could not cajole
Though full adept - yet would not rob
Thy hands the furnished bowl
He was God's son - I have no doubt!
The things I saw that day
The crowd so easily you could rout
Ye let them have their say
Still in my head I hear the noise
Flogged my orders He
Then removed His purple guise
And dragged to Calvary

The Nazarine! The Nazarine!
My life fore then was free
The Nazarine! The Nazarine!
The burden placed on me!
'Twould seem like I events that day
Impressed upon thy soul
The years gone by when sent away
Whatever be thy role
I long suspect though kept alive
Like me the odds were slim
Makes us aware - the truth derive
Our fates because of Him.

Thomas Ritchie

Jesus Will Then Love You Even More

You may have a tragic fate
Or some problems with your weight
Perhaps you haven't got a job or home
You may have a foul disease
Be in debt up to your knees
You may be short and ugly like a gnome
If you lost a limb or two
You have reasons to feel blue
Maybe your mom-in-law has come to stay
If your marriage seems to fail
If your brother goes to jail
If you believe your only son is gay

Then remember - God has told you - don't despair
If you're bothered by too much to bear
If you're plagued by sufferings galore
Jesus will then love you even more

If some hoodlums stole your car
Thank your God that you still are
Safe and sound while riding in a train
If your health will soon decay
'Cause you smoke a lot each day
The good Lord brings you comfort in your pain
If your ticker is worn out
If your joints are full of gout
If earthquakes crushed your garden and your house
If you lose your teeth and hair
And have tumours here and there
And if your best friend came and stole your spouse.

Then remember - God has told you - don't despair
If you're bothered by too much to bear
If you're plagued by sufferings galore
Jesus will then love you even more.

Ivar Kalleberg

Easter Story

A divine purpose for Your birth
The redemption of sinners here on Earth
To bear our sins in a mortal frame
Obedient in death, ignoring the shame

Beaten mercilessly, scourged and jeered
A crown of thorns to grace Your head
Sweat like blood dripped all around
A humble lamb in whom no guile was found

Cursed is anyone who hangs on a tree
In unconditional love, Jesus died for me
On an old rugged cross You were crucified
Amid two thieves on either side

You arose from the grave in victory
An empty tomb bears testimony
The disciples saw Your nail pierced hands
My Risen Saviour the Son of Man

Through Your death, burial and resurrection
Every man inherits the gift of salvation
When we repent our sins are forgiven
In baptism You adopt us as Your children

As dear children our lights must shine through
Help us to be mindful of the things we do
Strengthen us as we watch and pray
Your imminent return seems closer each day

Every knee shall bow
Every tongue confess
Before our Lord and Saviour Jesus Christ
The king of righteousness.

Maxine A Forrester

Easter

Easter, is a time of year
Part of the Christian calendar.
It falls sometimes in March or maybe April
Had ignorant ancients, held in wonder.

The story told is that a saviour
Was crucified and raised from the dead
By a power outside our understanding
This miracle is worship-ped.

The story tells of thirteen men
Sitting around a supper table
The saviour with wine and breaking bread
Shares symbolically His blood and body, while He's able.

He tells them that one of their group has sold Him
And thirty pieces of silver holds
Judas knew he was the guilty one
And hid his face in the table folds.

He says one amongst them will thrice deny Him
But they all say it can't be true.
Later, Peter in Gethsemane's garden does
Is mortified his Saviour knew.

The real meaning behind this story
Is to give us all hope no matter what life brings
To forgive and to love one another
To give our souls Heaven sent wings.

Sheila Bates

Bible Story

A pure white bible, cross embossed,
shines in the sun, left behind on a stair.
Where has it come from? Who left it there?
Dare I take it? Oh yes, I dare!

No sudden thunderbolt zaps
my cobblestone steps
as they clip the still Sunday air
Which is hardly moved at all,
for it's too soon yet for a Sunday stressed
by heavier sounds of progress.

So this Easter's doubly spiced,
what with hot cross buns and a stolen Bible.
Then sweet crazy pavings of chocolaty curves
are served up clutches for me and my friends
as we tot up our eggs again and again
and sing dreamy hymns to a green hill far away
where Easter bunnies nibble
on this lazy, endless day.

That was long ago.
Like somebody before me, somewhere
sometime on the way to now,
I lost that pure white Bible.
I wonder - where did it go?

Eileen Caiger Gray

Maytime

Since you have no more room for me in your heart,
I hope, at least, your mind holds a niche
Where I may creep in and hide
Gentle dust will soon mantle me over.

A day many come when this new love
Will lose its flavour and become sour;
And distraught, and writhing with a great distaste
Of life, you shake me out of my hiding place;
I will try to easy your pain,
As we recall our Maytime happiness
And hopefully, with real love, we will
        Walk that golden path again.

Mary Frances Mooney

God Bless You

'God bless you,' said the rich man
with so little thought
he has much wealth and power
much more than he ought.
His mind is taken over
with thoughts of goods and store
his greed is so demanding
he must get more and more.

'God bless you,' said the poor man,
he meant it as a prayer
he stood shaking in a doorway
his bones were almost bare.
He had nothing else to offer,
nothing else to give.
He had no wealth or power,
nor even a place to live.

Which of these words are priceless,
which would you prefer to keep?
The thoughtless word of the rich man
or those said with feelings deep?

William Ahern

Emmaus Revisited

Didn't our hearts just burn within us
As He walked beside us on the way?
Didn't we feel His living presence
On this glorious Easter day?

The hills may rise up steep before us
The light may vanish from our lives.
But He will always walk beside us
Our companion and our guide.

Bernard Fyles

Spring's Promise

Springtime's promises unfold
Catkins shake their tails in glee
Daffodils dance in the breeze
Young lambs skip on wobbly knees.

Trees and flowers bud and bloom
Warm sunshine dispelling gloom
Gentle showers fall like tears
Refreshed hope, dispelling fears.

Springtime bringing new delight
Christ is Risen, Christ the Light
Time of thought, meditation,
Jesus died, our salvation.

Christ promised He'd rise again
Defeating death, sin and pain,
As the stone is rolled away
Joy breaks forth on Easter Day.

Springtime's promises abound
Birdsong trilling, thrilling sound.
Renewed every living thing
Hearts uplifted with the spring.

Joan Heybourn

Believe

Not alone in losing someone very dear
I find myself believing that they are always near
Deep in my heart I know they are all around
It is just a feeling as there is no sound
Wishful thinking to many I know it seems
But life is so wonderful locked in our dreams
In turn our memories get us through each day
To prevent us from despair and losing our way
Our lives so important as we share everything
Each day so special, what will it bring?
Happy thoughts and expectations as each day we face
Remembering always to go at one's own pace
Our loved ones now share all our ups and downs
So look for the good and ban any frowns
Remember with happiness how good life has been
Your life now has guidance form one not seen
Belief is the key to help mend a broken heart
We need this to stay strong as each day does start
So smile at the thought of happy days ahead
You are not alone there is no more to be said.

Anne Sackey

Potters House Christian Fellowship

P eople together united by love
O f our Saviour from above
T ogether on Wednesdays and Sundays for church
T ogether at night, joined after work
E veryone equal in the Lord's eyes
R egardless of creed, colour and ethnicity
S aved and washed in the blood

H olloway, Luton, Walthamstow too
O ur church locations to name but a few
U p north in Bolton, to the coast Southampton
S ome churches in London, Bromley and Brixton are two
E ven in Watford, too many to name, it's true.

Teri Manning

After The Visit

A fairy placed upon a tree where lights were shining bright
Present wrapped to hide away until the eve of night.
The morning comes with shouts of glee
Is one hiding there for me?

The children gather around the scene
Thinking Santa Claus has been
Their eager hands, the wrappers torn
Faces shining bright this morn.

Then when all have gone and played
You lay down softly feeling frayed
Now the day is over, you sit and ponder why
You used most of your savings on things you had to buy.

John Barker

Fulfillingness

Fulfillingness . . .
    What a kind and fragile word
It comes to me on a golden breeze
    And it means a lot, I've heard.
I could say it speaks with love to me
    Or ignore it if I choose,
But unfulfilled is a bitter pill
    That if swallowed makes you blue.
Fulfillingness . . .
    To claim it is my right,
To lay in its arms
    Is to bathe in the sun
    And to sleep with a peace in the night.
I have no wish for the torture
    For a life with a pulse I can't feel,
I stand at the crossroads to Heaven
    Walk with me,
        Show me fulfilled.

Andrew Hobbs

East And West

East, where the clerics
gather at dawn
and preach to the
shaded hearts of man.
Where chandeliers and trees in
blossom are the
firmament under which
souls are ransomed
for Persian roses,
whispering in the breeze.
They speak of senoritas far away
dwelling in Andalusian hills.
Where unity and balance reverberate
from the troubadour's strings
and one's first duty is to
the nurtured soul
polished and alive
encircled by seekers
and a mirror for us all
husband, child, mother, wanderer
who may just set us on fire
with an astral love
and a wisdom
that burns up the intellect
lights the mosque at night
and consoles all lovers
who must learn
how to share God's touch
casting jealousy aside
knowing that to burn is
enough for love to handle
old or young.
Eastern cleric or
senorita of the west.

John Hobbs

A Rose Unfolds

Green spear tipped palisade
Surrounded and protected
The promise of life within
Swelling and preparing for its task.
At first, a blushing hint,
Then daily, emerging slowly,
Until the tight wrapped bud
Stood in softest tones of dawn's awakening.
Each petal unfolded stealthily,
Graceful as a dancer's gesture,
A soft enticing path of welcome
For insects role in procreation.
The centre's sweetness was the lure,
Gifting in return dust of pollen
For visitors to spread abroad,
Completing thus nature's cycle.
In days of sun the roses glory
Was lifted high in tribute and thanks,
But rain's teardrops bowed the head
Mourning wasted time when no insects flew.
Rose's store exhausted, calyx swelling,
The bright dress of petals gently fell
Until no more were left,
Their time of living well completed.
So often have I stood entranced,
As each individual Creator's masterpiece
In pre-ordained progression,
Brought beauty affirming a life to come.

Di Bagshawe

Life Eternal And Infinite

Far outside the Earth's atmosphere and that of its moon
Our Milky Way galaxy spins round with our sun and planets
A fiery sun which gives us heat and light - providing the molecules
Which form to give a multitude of living things in our midst.

Nightly inky blackness punctured by uncountable points of light
Each illuminated particle aged by light years in perpetual space.
Beaming their rays from long ago - travelling backwards in time.
Galaxies of space objects, evolve into stars, planets and such
Dark matter - that is beyond our comprehension.

Black holes that emit no light, red dwarfs - glowing dying embers
Whilst new exploding bodies herald their star's birth.
Nothing is lost forever it just changes form and composition.
Life eternal and infinite.

Helen Sarfas

A Rainbow Of Umbrellas

Sitting in a row feet dangling free
Downwards to the azure sea
Only feet and umbrellas form the scene
While giggling twitches the umbrella screen.

Yellow, pink, orange green, red
All shade from sun a shapely head.
Minds are left to imagine the scene
As the giggling twitches the umbrella screen.

Picture the picture, focus your mind
As these five girls sit and unwind.
Bare feet are swinging, no hands are seen
Hidden behind the umbrella's screen.

A boat is swishing on one side
And silver fish silently glide.
The pier is empty save for this scene
Just giggling twitching the umbrella screen.

Pamela Sears

Lifting The Veil

Eastertide reminds us of God, our Father's love
He sent his only Son to Earth from the happy realms above
Jesus came to Earth a tiny babe and grew up just like us
Met with every kind of man, so many lives He touched
His Father guided every step He took upon the way
How proud He must have been to see His progress day by day
Jesus grew up in a humble home, a carpenter to trade
Never looked for earthly riches nor any claim to fame
Yet he taught so many people about the love of God
They followed Him in thousands, people flocked to hear His words
He healed so many sick or maimed, and those who could not see
Yet he only lived a few short years till the age of thirty-three!
His young life was taken wantonly by those He sought to save
His body laid to rest within a lonely borrowed grace.
But Jesus overcame death's sting and now He lives again
Enthroned with God the Father within the heavenly realms.
Death is not an eraser, His words and deeds live on
And if we believe and love Him we can live with Him in Heaven
He died that we might be forgiven all our mortal sin
Open up your heart, believe, ask Him to enter in.
He paid the price for all of us, accept the gift on offer
At Easter the veil between time and eternity thins to gossamer.

Maureen Quirey

Early Today

Early today, close by the border of night's dream, a thrush sang
Through thinning darkness before dawn I heard his song repeat.
Insistently he sang, scattering remnants of soft sleep,
Commanding me, 'Awake, awake.'

The moon hung full and white above dark trees
And he had come this time, clear voiced on frost air,
Above snowdrops massed where in the snow he'd fed:
So thankful then for meagre gifts.

Now, on season's cusp, he has returned to calm domain
And share this benediction to the spring.

Patrick Osada

Windows

W intry views
I lluminous hues
N ew church pews
D iminishing mews
O n stage cues
W ithstanding news
S hopping queues.

Ramandeep Kaur

A Wedding

My daughter's getting married
Such a lovely surprise
Seeing her try on wedding gowns
It bought happy tears to my eyes.

She's made her choice
Of a nice young man
They have their new home
And many future plans.

The bridesmaids have been chosen
The families are all due
The flowers are to be delivered
The speeches are written too.

I hope their special day goes well
And they treasure it for life
I know they will have photographs
Of the day they became husband and wife.

It makes me feel so very proud
To see our girl succeed
In making her perfect choice in life
See her love with such a need.

Jennifer Collins

So Close To Spring

Branches bend, pinging
Against the pane
Bowing and scraping
To March's gales.

Honour due, honour paid
Nature promises
Softer days ahead

She keeps her pledge
Redeems her debt
With yellow dancing daffodils.

Sheila O'Hara

Anniversary

A day to remember
A time to rejoice
Good foundations
A written voice.

A celebration day
New challenges found
A time to reflect
Ideas sound.

A winning formula
Good teams portray
In rhyme or reason
A basic forté.

Words of comfort
Something I'd guess
A house of laughter
Frequently, no less.

As the years roll by
We must change
Keeping pace
A healthy range.

Pauline Pickin

Not Our Wish

When our honey bees feel weak at the knees
and so cannot pollinate any more
ever more jelly fish enter our seas
to swish along and sting us by our shore.

For week after week the rain down-pelting
but all those jellyfish could not care less
(Unlike polar bears whose ice is melting)
for theirs is a realm rising and restless.

Even basking sharks who swallow plankton
well know that humans over fish their sea,
When, on land, elephant and tiger gone
just like our vital fertilising bee
then people now obsessed by Credit Crunch
may discover tomorrow there's no lunch!

No bees, no crops, no us, it's not our wish
to let our world belong to jelly fish.

Christine Mary Creedon

Of All The Places

For centuries the village inn
A haven for travellers
Coach and horses to rest
Nostalgia in the old oak beams
Ceiling so low and sawdust floors
Barrels of ale and lamplight
Casting shadows making a glow
Ghosts of the past.

Still the local boasts its appeal
Sometimes quaint, sometimes new
Familiar friendly atmosphere prevails
Tradition for always never fails
Ageless, somewhere to meet
Good company and a drink to enjoy
Spirits of our time.

Joy Milligan

If You Dream

If you dream you will know
But if you don't know
You will drain away
Some things should always be bright green
If you adorn your dream
You will never slip up
Tomorrow will bring flowers
Your baskets and vases wait for
When the players play
You can watch keenly
And when your nightmares depart
You can dream and sing
If you dream you will find
That which you sought so madly
And I can only watch from here
And pray you reach your Heaven.

Muhammad Khurram Salim

Three Gold Rings

Three gold rings on the table
Generations of love in a velvet box
Where have they been?
What have they seen?

Now they are here
Forever
The memories hold true
Faces in a crowd
All are gone now
But not forgotten.

You are married next week
It' your turn to fly the flag for love
Never let people hurt you
Love has its own destiny
You are made for each other.

Kenneth Mood

Rainbow Of Despair

Yesterday
I fell asleep,
Daydreaming of the world
When in my eyes
All colours run
And rainbows
Filled the empty skies.

Enclosed in pain,
Trapped by love,
Each band
Encircled
From above.

As I watched they began to peel,
Their hearts, to me in truth revealed.

Red, was full of rage
Each time, he watched the world,
Whilst orange showed obsession,
That quarrelsome man observed.
Green, demonstrates the greed
That man, parades with ease
And bitter blue, the loathing
Then feeds its sister's greed.
Indigo-faced, injustice
That the world would never solve.
As violet, oozed its vileness
At a world where love grows cold.

Enclosed in pain,
Trapped by love,
Each band
Encircled
From above.

As the panorama faded
I found myself aware
If man would learn to do the same?
What beauty could we share?

Alvin Creighton

Happiness Is . . .

The dawn of each new day
Warm comfort in the bath
A traffic free highway
To know fun and to laugh.

A Christmas snowy white
A roaring logwood fire
The glow of candlelight
With carols from a choir.

A winter, day and mild
Relaxing as day ends.
To hold a newborn child
To drink champagne with friends.

The gift of a bouquet
The first lambs seen in spring
To eat a crème brûlée
To hear dawn's chorus sing.

Blue skies without a cloud
Plans made without a hitch
A moment feeling proud
Dark chocolate, smooth and rich.

A fragrant flower's perfume
To touch, to hear, to see.
Sun shining in my room
When writing poetry.

This gift of life we share
To give love and to show it
The time to stand and stare
To be loved and to know it.

Joy Saunders

Picasso

Sitting I sight the looking tree of what is
And yet no form in realities garden partakes to action the
                                           lingering brush
Inwardly seeking for spirits voice, I conjure stokes parallel form
And yet, am I to become self importance own reflection, or should
                                       I stop before reflections end
In truth is it my loneliness that treads unforgiving fear deep into my soul
Yet I would like to think, I cannot help what I perceive, what I feel,
                                     even what I have become
For the word has become all, and all the work, in the end,
The self painting of characters own make-up
So I wait for the next mask, to action the hand of pallets eye,
                                        to create other form.

S Beattie

By Example

How small and trusting is the child
Watching every move we're making
Emulating all his elders, always giving, never taking
If we always strive to be, ever gentle, loving, caring,
Surely he will also grow with boundless love forever sharing
Don't blame the youth for all his ways
If we fill all his younger days
With scenes of striking and rebelling
Harsh words and actions all repelling
When hope is lost or so it seems
The child then starts to plan his dreams
So in the end, the youth then can
Make all his dreams become a plan.

Patricia Taylor

Cupboards

My cupboards are standing tall guarding
What are they guarding?
Why my books, my thoughts, my life!
Everything I have ever done
Prepared a lesson or given a party,
Made a game, or written an essay.

Of course what I should really like is a studio
A place designed to foster creativity
A place where I could establish order
And keep it, for here I am always compromising
Trying to make things fit when they don't want to
Because this is really my dining room.

But everyone has learned to live with me
My untidiness and my unorthodox housekeeping
Even the dog keeps quiet when I am writing!
It is a blessed escape
For as soon as I venture into the kitchen
He will follow me and demand a walk!

Barbara Tozer

Sightings

Be seeing you in the springtime
When the sails turn for home

Be seeing you in the summer
When the barley is mown

Be seeing you at autumn
When leaf fall hides the rain

Be seeing you in winter
Always once more again.

Paul Thompson

The Baton Of Life

How can nature be so beautiful when fate can be so cruel?
It's such an empty feeling when the road ahead looks lonely.
But then I stopped, looked down, it was shining like a jewel,
A dew-covered crocus standing proud, the one and only.
How did she come to be here on her own, is that not cruel?
Then she seemed to speak to me through poems in my memory.

She showed an inner peace and a strong feeling of survival,
I could feel her colour 'mauve' it filled me with her wisdom
As it drifted deep inside me, it said, listen, I'll tell you all.
I am the baton of life as you are and your children's children.
We are all here to learn, you and I know we're more than able
So be strong, move along but please come back and see us often.

Rosalin Harvey

Ribbons

I drift back
Some forty years
The singer leaving me in tears.

Words of a little girl in prayer
Requesting ribbons,
Scarlet ribbons for her hair.

So easy to forget good lost
Too long alone
And drowned by tears.

Memories melt
My frozen heart
Returning childhood
On lost dreams.

As for a while I picture near
My mother as she combs my hair . . .

Anita Richards

Cefn Lea

Rumours in various lights glint
glaring at my eyes in return as each wink defies
my eyes a-glow at navy air.
Alone upon the bed of snow
staring up at every agenda.
Star upon star upon star
afar on some planet, journeying towards impending implosion.
Eroded earth beneath my chilly feet
tonight the sky is mine,
in a blanket waved about my head
I cannot see it all at once
before the cloudy smugglers rain above.
The string eyes of heaven's face
erase all air.

Time stands still and as we,
me and He
both awe together at such beauty.
I fall upon the snowy ground
astounded in a loving touch
by all the earth
but most of all the stars.

Lozi Bolton

Ask Yourself

You don't know what you've lost till it's lost
Then, you can't try hard enough to find it
You won't be satisfied until you try to retrieve it
If you do manage to pick up the pieces in the end
Ask yourself, was it *really* worth it?

Nayyar Shabbir Ahmad

Coincidence

We barely touched earth fruits
as we entered life together
each in different places
under the same sky.

Neither would remember,
but destiny ensured our paths crossed
and when we met
something stirred deep inside.

A longing touched our souls
that was never to be erased.
There was so question of who,
why or what
as hand in hand we walked
into the future under a turquoise sky.

Rosaleen Clarke

Years Gone By

Where are all those years gone
Since I was young?
Where are my youthful looks?
My puppy loves
All my youthful runs
Immature charm.
When I could skip and run
Now I cannot hardly walk.
Of past youthful experiences
Memories, one can only talk and talk.
Where are all these years gone?
Impossible to count everyone.
In my sunset years
Memories one youth
Memories of my youth rejoice
My age don't let me
Give me any choice.

Bryan George

Love On Call

There are woodlands where I'll go
whenever life finds me feeling low,
have only to pause beneath a tree,
let its branches re-work our history

I'll feel the pull of Memory Lane
to a peace of mind, away from pain,
among the lines in your kind face,
subtle comforts of a warm embrace

I'll hear wise words you'd pass on
though but rarely heeding them then,
an impatient child (even grown)
anxious to be seen holding my own

I'll watch songbirds in a leafy sky,
images of a grace that will never die
though winter come and nature rest
till that renewal love pleads we trust

There are woodlands where I'll go
whenever life finds me feeling low,
have only to pause beneath a tree,
let its branches re-work our history

Sleep well. Hear Earth Mother's call
who can but make of it what we will

Roger Taber

Forward Press Information

We hope you have enjoyed reading this book - and that you will continue to enjoy it in the coming years.

If you like reading and writing poetry drop us a line, or give us a call, and we'll send you a free information pack.

Alternatively if you would like to order further copies of this book or any of our other titles, then please give us a call or log onto our website at
www.forwardpress.co.uk

**Forward Press Ltd. Information
Remus House
Coltsfoot Drive
Peterborough
PE2 9JX
(01733) 898101**